LIVERPOOL
JOHN MOORES UNIVERSITY
AVRIL ROBARTS LRC
TITHEBARN STREET
LIVERPOOL L2 2ER
TEL. 0151 231 4022

POST-NATAL DEPRESSION

The transition to motherhood is a challenging time in a woman's life, changing her relationships, her body, her identity, her behaviour and her future life prospects. Women are expected to adapt to the role of mother without protest, with positive emotions and with little disturbance to their own lives and those around them.

Post-Natal Depression challenges the expectation that it is normal to be a 'happy mother'. While as many as 90% of new mothers get anxious and depressed at some time in the early weeks and months of motherhood, the majority have personal explanations that challenge the traditional expert view that childbirth is the trigger and the biology of early motherhood is the cause of their problems. Unlike most traditional accounts of post-natal depression, this book does not pathologise what are in fact social rather than biological issues, but emphasises what women say about their experiences. Paula Nicolson sets women's accounts alongside expert evidence, and provides a radical critique of the traditional medical and social science explanations of post-natal depression. She supplies a systematic feminist psychological analysis of women's experiences following childbirth and argues that, far from being an abnormal, undesirable, pathological condition, it is a normal, healthy response to a series of losses.

Paula Nicolson is Senior Lecturer in Health Psychology at the Sheffield School for Health and Related Research, Sheffield University. Her previous publications include *Gender, Power and Organization* (1996), *Female Sexuality* (1994; edited with Precilla Choi), and *Gender Issues in Clinical Psychology* (1992; edited with Jane Ussher).

WITHDRAWN

- 5 OCT 2005

D0234962

WOMEN AND PSYCHOLOGY
Series Editor: Jane Ussher
Dept of Psychology, University College London

This series brings together current theory and research on women and psychology. Drawing on scholarship from a number of different areas of psychology, it bridges the gap between abstract research and the reality of women's lives by integrating theory and practice, research and policy.

Each book addresses a 'cutting edge' issue of research, covering such topics as post-natal depression, eating disorders, theories and methodologies.

The series provides accessible and concise accounts of key issues in the study of women and psychology, and clearly demonstrates the centrality of psychology to debates within women's studies or feminism.

The Series Editor would be pleased to discuss proposals for new books in the series.

Other titles in this series:

THE MENSTRUAL CYCLE
Anne E. Walker

RE-THINKING ABORTION
Mary Boyle

THE THIN WOMAN
Helen Malson

POST-NATAL DEPRESSION

Psychology, science and the transition
to motherhood

Paula Nicolson

LIVERPOOL
JOHN MOORES UNIVERSITY
AVRIL ROBARTS LRC
TITHEBARN STREET
LIVERPOOL L2 2ER
TEL 0151 231 4022

London and New York

First published 1998
by Routledge
11 New Fetter Lane, London EC4P 4EE

Simultaneously published in the USA and Canada
by Routledge
29 West 35th Street, New York, NY 10001

© 1998 Paula Nicolson

Typeset in Baskerville by
Ponting–Green Publishing Services,
Chesham, Buckinghamshire
Printed and bound in Great Britain by
Clays Ltd, St. Ives PLC

All rights reserved. No part of this book may be reprinted or
reproduced or utilised in any form or by any electronic,
mechanical, or other means, now known or hereafter
invented, including photocopying and recording, or in any
information storage or retrieval system, without permission in
writing from the publishers.

British Library Cataloguing in Publication Data
A catalogue record for this book is available
from the British Library

Library of Congress Cataloging in Publication Data
Nicolson, Paula.
Post-natal depression: psychology, science, and the transition to
motherhood / Paula Nicolson
p.   cm. – (Women and psychology)
Includes bibliographical references and index.
1. Postpartum depression.   2. Puerperal psychoses.
3. Women–Adjustment disorders.   4. Motherhood.
I. Title.   II. Series.
RG852.N53   1998

618.7'6–dc21   97–49218

ISBN 0–415–16362–5 (hbk)
ISBN 0–415–16363–3 (pbk)

— chapters to use

CONTENTS

TABLES

ACKNOWLEDGEMENTS

I want to thank the women who took part in this research, originally for my Ph.D. thesis, almost ten years ago. Without their time and co-operation neither the thesis nor the book would exist. I also thank those who helped me contact the participants and write up the study in its different forms, particularly Georgina Ray, Gill Bergstrand, Sharon Wallach, David Jones and Bram Oppenheim.

Since then I have been influenced by many friends and colleagues interested in qualitative research, the psychology of women and women's health. I particularly want to mention Karen Collins, Mavis Kirkham and Jane Ussher, who read and discussed the draft with me, and Kate Nicolson, without whom I probably would never have thought about any of this.

INTRODUCTION

… we end up dividing mothers into the good and containing, about whom nothing more needs to be said or done, and the mothers who require explaining. It is hard, but crucial to hold on to the idea of mothers as necessarily ambivalent.

(Parker, 1995: 99)

We tend to think in terms of the ever-present all-providing mother who anticipates the needs of her infant, supported by an ever-present, all-providing state which is also engaged in the process of ministering to the needs of children in the light of modern belief and knowledge.

(Dally, 1982: 87)

Notions of biological maternity and female physiology justified the association of women with nature in position to culture; they designated a woman's place within the family, the most basic biological and social unit.

(Moscucci, 1993: 4)

The transition to motherhood is a challenging time in a woman's life and motherhood is a state to which a large proportion of women aspire. This is the case despite evidence that mothering is a hard job which can never be done to perfection. Motherhood is also a role that receives decreasing support from government sources in western industrial societies, although these are the very communities where traditional support from extended family networks may no longer be relied upon. To progress from non-mother to mother, or from mother of one child to mother of more than one, changes a woman's relationships, her body, her identity, her behaviour and her future life prospects. It is an intensely personal experience. ✦Motherhood is also a public experience in that 'mother' is a prescribed social role and identity, and the process of pregnancy, labour, childbirth, child-care and development are the focus of professional endeavour for doctors, midwives, health visitors, psychologists and social workers. These experts prescribe the motherhood role with impunity and apparently without question.

The consequences of this are clear: discourses surrounding childbirth and motherhood position the role of 'mother' as biological and immutable. Childbirth and motherhood, exclusively the function of the female body, in both a physical and social sense, are seen to be natural for women. Women have the

1

capacity to become pregnant and give birth so it automatically follows that they 'know' how to care for and rear children. Thus, it is believed that women will want both to become mothers and to mother 'well'.

This implies that women adapt to the role of mother without protest, exhibiting positive emotional reactions, with little disturbance to their own lives and those of their close companions. The medical and popular discourses surrounding childbirth reflect these irrefutable beliefs about women's 'nature', capabilities and behaviour. As Ann Oakley observed some years ago, 'cultural femininity and biological reproduction are curiously synonymous in the proclamations of medical science about women' (Oakley, 1980: 50).

Despite this, significant numbers of women in western society who become mothers fail to make the transition smoothly. Between one-third and up to 90% are estimated to experience emotional disturbance, anxiety and depression in the days, weeks and months after childbirth: identified in research and clinical accounts as 'post-natal depression'.

But what is post-natal depression? The term encapsulates a mixture of meanings to different interest groups and raises significant questions for practitioners and scientists working in the context described above where motherhood, in the absence of major health or financial difficulties, is expected to be more or less trouble-free.

In this book I explore how the concept of post-natal depression (PND) represents disparate meanings for the vested interests of the groups who employ it. For instance, primary care workers such as general practitioners or health visitors need to find a diagnosis which describes and explains the symptoms such as tiredness, unhappiness or the inability to cope with the demands of child-care that many new mothers present to them. The women themselves sometimes need to label their adverse feelings towards their lives now taken up with infant care. It may be hard to understand how the reality of motherhood for them seems to contradict the anticipated joy of having a baby or child. The scientists, trained within the traditional medical model, often feel compelled to seek objective, clearly measurable phenomena with intrinsically recognisable signs and symptoms.

However, despite increasing research efforts directed at predicting and preventing PND, very little research has focused specifically upon women's own accounts of either what the transition to motherhood feels like for them, or how they themselves explain their emotional states and the changes in those states. It was this that intrigued me when I began reviewing the literature for this research, and subsequently underpinned my attempts to provide a different perspective on the concept of PND. Very simply, I wanted women to explain what they believed was happening to them.

This book is based upon a series of in-depth interviews with women through the transition to motherhood. It attempts to develop a systematic, scientific explanation of post-natal depression, building upon women's accounts of their experiences while critically examining both quantitative studies and the approach I myself adopted using in-depth interviews. It is still the case that no-one has got it right – but it is important for women, scientists, clinicians and lay understanding of the experience of becoming a mother that both subjective and objective knowledge is taken seriously.

Psychologists' ideas about women's reproductive health have developed a higher profile since I completed the thesis in 1988. Since then the psychology of women, feminist theories and qualitative research have all become notable players within the discipline. Nevertheless, an intellectual chasm still exists between women's experiences and what counts as science.

In this book I identify the principal reasons for this problematic relationship and demonstrate, through the research interviews I have conducted, that women's experiences need to be taken more seriously if knowledge informing clinical practice in this area is to be effective in alleviating the distress of women during the transition to motherhood.

The outline is as follows: Chapter 1, 'Women's experience of motherhood', examines women's lives as mothers. It explores why women become mothers and draws attention to the contrast between scientific beliefs about the motherhood role, the maternal instinct and the experience of caring for children. It argues that the role of the expert in relation to motherhood and child-care has further burdened women by charging them with the responsibility for ensuring the mental and physical well-being of their partners and children, and co-operating with health professionals.

Chapter 2 explores the 'Competing explanations of post-natal depression', to provide a critical review of the mainstream literature on PND. It identifies the development of the contemporary clinical framework and points out the rationale and consequences for women when 'post-natal depression' is explained through female biology. The female body is portrayed as a faulty machine, which in some cases fails because of hormonal problems and in others because of historical or congenital psychological defects. Having a baby is essentially a biological and clinical experience which can either be 'put right' after dysfunction or the dysfunction be prevented.

Chapter 3, 'The context of post-natal depression', further explores the theoretical implications derived from the discussions in Chapters 1 and 2 through a focus on the psychological experience of becoming a mother. It places this experience beyond the entirely biological to within the context of a woman's biography, where gender power relations and subjective experience are crucial. The chapter draws upon the work of symbolic interactionist and phenomenological theorists as well as contemporary feminist sociologists and psychologists. It questions the concept of a 'normal' reaction to childbirth and the post-natal period.

In Chapter 4, 'Post-natal care and "maternity blues"', the contrast between feminist and medical models of childbirth and the 'baby blues' are set alongside the respondents' accounts of their own experiences of labour and delivery.

Chapter 5, 'Reflexivity, intervention and the construction of post-natal depression', places the emphasis on the way the research process itself is crucial for explaining how women understand the way becoming a mother places them in relation to the role and the PND discourses. It argues that traditional psychology, which takes the 'experimenters' and their wishes out of the research equation, is misguided. Effective and convincing science is more complex – counting the researcher and research process 'in'.

Chapter 6, 'Loss, happiness and post-natal depression: the ultimate paradox', focuses upon women's reports of the transition to motherhood and how having a baby means a sense of change which is primarily experienced as loss – loss of physical integrity, time, sexuality, work, status, autonomy, male company and many other aspects of life. The model employed by Peter Marris, which involves loss and reintegration as a natural part of human psychological development and maturation, is used to argue that depression after childbirth is better understood as a time when mourning is normal and healthy, leading to psychological reintegration.

Finally, Chapter 7, 'Knowledge, myth and the meaning of post-natal depression', explores what is useful about the concept of 'post-natal depression' in the context of critical, feminist psychology. What have clinicians and clinical researchers learnt about women's reproductive lives by studying PND? Why haven't the challenges to the traditional approach to this issue been taken seriously? I examine the potential impact on women's lives of a feminist psychology which challenges the concept of PND and contrast this with the mainstream clinical approach which offers a label, removes blame and promises cure. Where does the future of research on PND lie?

Profiles of the respondents, outlined along with tables of their reproductive histories and social status, as well as details of the methodology, are appended.

1

WOMEN'S EXPERIENCE OF MOTHERHOOD

> I still can't think of myself as a mother, even when she's there. I can't think of her as mine – my daughter ... but I do think of her as mine, but not of myself as a mother. Do you know what I mean? It's quite difficult to believe ... I think it takes a while to sink in.
>
> (Jane)[1]

> I still can't seem to feel as a mummy with a capital 'M'. I just can't seem to get into that. Sometimes I lie in bed and think about it and think 'God I'm her mum'. But I don't feel anyone but Penelope. But I know she's my daughter and I find that frightening and exciting.
>
> (Penelope)

Introduction

The words above, spoken one month after their daughters' births, demonstrate the contradictory ways in which individual women experience having their own baby, caring for that baby and understand the social meaning of mothers and mothering.

This chapter examines what it is like to be a mother – particularly since motherhood remains central to women's lives despite social and economic change. It explores why women become mothers and focuses upon the contrasts between scientific beliefs about the motherhood role, the maternal instinct and the experience of caring for children.

The experience of motherhood

> How beautiful and important it is for a woman to have a child. When you get married in Africa it's also emphasised that it is for children. It's not like a duty – it's part and parcel of being married.
>
> (Matilda)

---

1 All the names of the participants have been changed. See their profiles in the appendices.

> The attention that a baby requires and the resulting fatigue are not always to the parents' liking. And in many cases parents do not pass the 'sacrifice test'.
>
> (Badinter, 1981: 39)

Patterns of fertility and the decision to become a mother have a complicated connection with women's lives overall. Better educated, middle-class women appear to have ensured greater control over when, if and how many children they have than have those women from less privileged backgrounds. Further, control over fertility means more scope for education and employment for women, which in turn provides opportunities for independence and autonomy. Statistics make it clear that more women in the 1990s were divorcing, separating, marrying later or not marrying at all, more frequently than was the case in the 1970s and 1980s, and these data are clearly connected to the fact that women's lives are no longer solely prescribed by their role as mother in the traditional family (see Gittins, 1993).

However, what women do and social beliefs about what women should do are sometimes at odds with each other. Motherhood and womanhood stand in a complex and contradictory relationship, despite the fact that this relationship appears to be changing. While motherhood is still central to women's identity, recent demographic changes appear to suggest that motherhood alone no longer dictates the pattern of women's lives, and may not be such a popular choice for women as it once was (Church and Sommerfield, 1995). Under patriarchy, however, motherhood has a mythological, mysterious and powerful status. Only women are granted this status, and it is one to which all women have been expected to aspire. The reality of mothers' lives, however, often fails to match these aspirations. Motherhood is a challenge; although potentially enjoyable, it is also hard work and routinely stressful (Richardson, 1993). It affects relationships with men and other women, and changes occupational, domestic and sexual arrangements.

> When people come round, I can't have a proper conversation. I used to notice it before I had him when other people could not give me attention. I'm doing the same things to my friends now! It's a bit irritating.
>
> (Jerri)

> Everything seems to revolve around him [the baby]. When Tom comes in I'm exhausted. We both look after him for a few hours and I go to bed and Tom stays up with him. I'm up first thing with him.
>
> (Jerri)

Becoming a mother often means economic dependence on another person or the state, and frequently reduces women's income. As Sylvia observes:

I now have to ask him for money. I don't like doing that ... I feel funny asking because I've not been in that position before. I had a house and a business and my own money. If I had money I'd spend it. If I didn't, I didn't. Even with the baby I feel guilty. I've said, 'We'll really have to buy a drop-sided cot and they're about fifty pounds dear'. I don't know why I feel I'm not contributing to the finances at the moment. I'm bringing up a baby – but it makes me feel guilty.

(Sylvia)

Being a mother influences social and personal identity, and has implications for women's health because of exhaustion and stress (Doyal, 1995). So, for example:

Everything gets out of proportion at the end of the day. I get a bit hysterical sometimes. It seems very rushed. I have to think about the meal and I have to wash up straight away.

(Hilary)

I'd have a day of baby and a day of cats running under my feet and then I'd discover the mess on the carpet and it was too much to cope with.

(Isobel)

... his crying for hours on end ... nothing could console him. We were both getting fractious about it as we were both missing an awful lot of sleep.

(Isobel)

Feminist analyses of the conditions surrounding motherhood have identified its socially prescribed situation as an accompaniment to marriage, heterosexuality, monogamy and economic viability (Gittins, 1993). But is motherhood still perceived as the key means of women's oppression in patriarchal societies, as many have argued (Bleier, 1984)? Do young working-class women still see it as a means of liberation from the prospect of dreary paid employment (Griffin, 1989)? Motherhood is more than anything a complex social role with ambiguous and potentially contradictory consequences for women.

Despite the prominence of motherhood as a social institution, and the almost universal expectation that women will become mothers, the everyday reality of mothering is frequently invisible. For women caught up in the myths that accompany motherhood, failure to achieve that imaginary status is frequently a shock (Parker, 1995). Women who do not have children are also caught in these contradictions and constraints. Women who are not mothers are seen as failed and unfeminine women, and achievements and pleasures gained outside motherhood are condemned within patriarchy as substitutes for normal femininity (Woollett, 1991). For women caught up in the myths that accompany motherhood, failure to achieve that imaginary status is frequently a 'shock' (Parker, 1995). IMPORTANT QUOTES

What is motherhood?

> I've been forced to realise that having a baby wasn't quite so unique, and because it was the central point of my life for so long, I've now been forced to realise that other people have done it. ... I don't know whether it's taken a whole dimension out of my life or added one!
>
> (Sharon)

Perceptions of mothers as powerful and influential and the romanticisation and idealisation of the mothering role (Apter, 1993) need to be qualified in the context of women's everyday experiences. Motherhood as an institution includes certain responsibilities and duties, but women's power is limited. Women's power in both the public and private/domestic spheres is subject to the rule of men – both as individuals and as represented by patriarchy. Psychologists have traditionally claimed priority for mothers' power over children, through emphasising the importance of mother–child relationships (Apter, 1993) and through the debate on mothers' responsibilities to their children (Tizard, 1991). However, legal and traditional power over women and children is held by men (Segal, 1990).

Matriarchy (defined as a society with matriarchal government and descent reckoned through female lineage) is not recognised in most societies and is certainly not a significant means of social organisation. Claims from community and anthropological studies that matriarchies prevail in certain traditional subcultures, for example among black urban American groups (Kitzinger, 1978) or among traditional white working-class communities in British cities (Young and Wilmott, 1966), cannot be upheld in terms of true power in contemporary western society. Ruth Bleier (1984), reviewing anthropological studies of a large number of cultures, argued that women's roles are always of a lower status to those of men, and this continues to be upheld through the enactment of gendered roles (Connell, 1993). In some small, non-industrial societies where men have primary responsibility for aspects of child-care, mothering is taken very seriously and given high status, which is not the case when women do it.

Most mothers in industrial and non-industrial, urban and rural, societies are oppressed. They may have particular responsibilities, but not the accompanying rights to choose how they mother or whether to mother at all. The popular perceptions of maternal influence and power are mythological and the origins of this myth lie within patriarchy. Its repercussions have had a powerful psychological effect on relationships between mothers and daughters, and affect expectations of mothering from generation to generation.

It is through the everyday experience of the mother–daughter relationship that the contradictions in the myth become clear: 'Belief in the all powerful mother spawns a recurrent tendency to blame the mother on the one hand, and a fantasy of maternal perfectibility on the other' (Chodorow and Contratto, 1982: 55). The romanticised and idealised woman, full of love, forgiveness and selflessness, does not and cannot exist, so that all mothers are destined to disappoint their children and themselves.

Mother-blaming occurs on a number of levels, from individual attributions to mothers as the cause of psychological insecurities to the portrayal of the cold, rejecting, neurotic or inadequate mother in popular culture (Sayers, 1988; Parker, 1995). The patriarchal myth of maternal power renders women culpable, and thus in reality deprives them of effective social influence. Women are consequently perceived as imperfect in their central role, while men as fathers can maintain their own mythological status and claim the admiration of their sons and daughters.

Science and motherhood

How is it, then, that mothers are 'blamed' and seen as both powerful and destructive? These contradictory images of motherhood are constructed and exploited within patriarchy through the medium of scientific knowledge. They operate to ensure that many aspects of motherhood are rendered invisible, and that women as mothers are denied the power to change this situation within existing social structures. The mechanisms through which the status of motherhood is controlled are both social and psychological. Motherhood is often idealised and some argue that men experience 'womb envy', that is, they envy women's ability to become pregnant and give birth (Erikson, 1975). The image of the idealised mother, however, exists in stark contrast to men's apparent unwillingness to become involved in the aspects of infant care that are available to them (Nicolson, 1990) and with the daily lives of the women attempting to mother (Parker, 1995).

The role of 'mother' has not evolved in a 'natural' way, nor is it outside culture and free from ideology. It has been socially constructed within patriarchy through a complex set of power relations which ensure that women become mothers and practise motherhood in narrowly defined ways. This is achieved in part through the mechanism of 'science', which bolsters existing power relations. Contemporary motherhood is the product of (at least) nineteenth- and twentieth-century medical/biological and psychological/social science, and this can be seen in a number of ways.

Social prescriptions for contemporary motherhood are constantly offered, reinforced and embellished by experts with recourse to science, and their versions of what constitutes good mothering practice is the socially received wisdom. Certain kinds of claims to knowledge are given priority over others, and it is those that serve the needs of the socially powerful (in this case, men) (Foucault, 1973; and Philp, 1985) that pass into popular discourse and come to represent our everyday understanding of what we all take for granted as truth or facts (Nicolson, 1993).

In the case of motherhood, while there are potentially a myriad dimensions which could be studied to explain and determine mothering practice (that is, the nature of the role itself, what behaviour is appropriate and so on), only a small proportion of what constitutes motherhood has been identified and described. In other words, *normative* behaviour associated with mothering has emerged from the power of the knowledge-claims of scientists which suit the needs of patriarchy (Foucault, 1973). These knowledge-claims have not only informed the ideology of mainstream social and psychological science but, more importantly, the every-day understanding that women have of themselves. This means that the accompanying stresses of motherhood may be experienced by women as their own inadequacies (Boulton, 1983; Lewis, 1995b).

I shall briefly explore some of these knowledge-claims and normative prescriptions, before identifying their manifestations in the social and psychological conditions of contemporary motherhood.

Experts and child-rearing: how to become a good mother

I felt so incompetent. It was as if we were making a right mess of it.

(Felicity)

It takes monumental powers of organisation in order to actually do anything … time just does disappear.

(Felicity)

I feel guilty because at the end of the day it's totally unproductive. I've got nothing to show for it apart from the baby.

(Sylvia)

The focus of experts on motherhood has been upon the effects of mothering on children, and the marital relationship, post-natal adjustment and when reproductive technology to aid fertility is appropriate. This clearly reflects the ideology underlying their claims to scientific knowledge. A number of ways have been suggested by these experts in which maternal behaviour can have potentially dire consequences for children, not only in their infancy and pre-school years, but also through adolescence and into adulthood. John Bowlby's assertions about the mothering role is a good example of this. Mother love in infancy, he claimed, is as important for mental health as vitamins and proteins are for physical health (Bowlby, 1951). Above all else, infants need mothers, and those mothers have to love them. This love, by implication, needs to be ever-available and offered without qualification, regardless of the mother's own needs and circumstances.

The consequent development of the 'maternal deprivation thesis' redefined the responsibilities of women towards their children, although the implications for women's lives were largely ignored. The emphasis in all this work was on the dependency needs of infants, and the psychological implications of separation traumas for the remainder of life. Mothers' needs were invisible.

Bowlby's thesis not only informed popular ideas about child-care, but also set the parameters for subsequent psychological research on infant/child development, adopting the notion of the 'secure base' as an ideal context for human development. This paradigm emerged as a moral as well as psychological prescription for mental health. The burden for providing the secure base fell upon mothers, regardless of circumstances and abilities (Ainsworth, 1992).

Evidence of the interconnection between science and politics can be seen in Denise Riley's (1983) study of women's work and day-care in the immediate post-war/post-Bowlby period:

> The reproductive woman at the heart of family policy was surrounded by the language of pronatalism. By pronatalism, I mean that despondency and alarm over the low birth rate, both past and as anticipated by demographers, which took the solution to the problem to be encouraging women to have more children; four per family was a widely agreed target.
>
> (Riley, 1983: 151)

Riley paints a complex picture, contrasting with some popular contemporary feminist images of women's post-war resistance to leaving the labour market (for example, as in the film *The Life and Times of Rosie the Riveter*). Many women, exhausted by the multiple burdens of child-care, domestic responsibility and work outside the home, appeared to welcome the pronatalist direction of government policy, which included ideas about the dangers for children of anything less than maternal dedication and constant availability. This was accomplished, at least in part, through direct information on film and in child-care manuals, for the specific consumption of women (Richardson, 1993), making it clear that experts know best, but also helping to ensure that women focused their major efforts upon mothering, or the management of mothering.

More recently, attention has been paid to the role of the father (see Chapter 6). However, the treatment of fatherhood by experts has been explained differently from the motherhood role. In clear contrast to mothers, fathers are represented as adding positive ingredients to the beleaguered and insufficient mother–child relationship. Fathers' involvement has traditionally been seen as improving children's intellectual and social capacities (Parke, 1981; McGuire, 1991). Mothers, it seems, are seen primarily as supplying the basic conditions for survival and maintenance, while experiencing a decline in their own wider personal capacities. Feminist studies of motherhood clearly show the ways in which the mothering role operates to exclude women's own development; for example, sometimes resulting in a self-defined sense of being unfit for tasks demanding intellectual skills (Kaplan, 1992).

> I've totally reorganised my life around him which is totally different from what I anticipated. I'd always thought that babies would jolly well do what everyone else wanted to do. If you wanted to go trekking up a

mountain or out to dinner, then a baby just had to follow. But the reality is quite different.

(Isobel)

I certainly found that I was much slower in writing things than I normally would have been and you constantly have interruptions and it's a struggle to keep up with what's going on elsewhere. It's much easier to turn on the television than to read a paper. That's been a struggle.

(Shirley)

Academic interest in fathers has led to a further strand of expert concern: the 'family'. Functionalist sociologists have in the past been concerned to divide and stratify family roles/functions in terms of gender and generation, portraying the family as a social microcosm, where women were seen as both dependent and nurturant in the home in relation to men and children, and nurturant and dependent in society (Parsons and Bales, 1953). Subsequent sociological studies, like mainstream psychology, focused upon motherhood as a role or as a variable in predicting marital satisfaction, and it was not until the publication of Hannah Gavron's *The Captive Wife* in 1966 that contemporary sociologists attempted to take women seriously as mothers. Even Elizabeth Bott's (1957) sensitive and influential study, which took class and gender into account, failed to identify and challenge the conditions surrounding women's role in the family and in relation to child-care.

Feminist analysis of the family has redefined the context within which domestic relationships are enacted, dispelling the myth of the traditional nuclear family unit. Single parenthood, domestic violence, divorce and lesbian parenting all indicate the need to re-evaluate the way experts define and prescribe women's lives (Gittins, 1993).

In contemporary mainstream psychology, expert attention to the family has focused upon the transition to motherhood, and the consequences of becoming a mother for reducing marital intimacy (Kaplan, 1992), for women's impaired physical attractiveness, and for women's rejection of what had been 'normal' pre-pregnancy sexual relations (Reamy and White, 1987; Nicolson, 1991), and for precipitating post-natal or maternal depression which is detrimental to child-rearing (Foreman, 1994). These issues have all been taken as indices through which good motherhood/wifehood might be assessed.

Within the social sciences and medicine, mainstream patriarchal values are still given the status of knowledge. Despite feminist critiques, feminist analyses or woman-focused studies (such as Gavron, 1966) are less often adopted into the mainstream and so have less impact on popular ideas and beliefs. However, patriarchal frameworks alone do not fully account for women's thinking about their own experience of motherhood. Women draw upon personal experience as well as popular discourses, and this often sets up the contradictions that potentially lead to feminist consciousness.

Becoming a mother

Motherhood is *not* a unitary experience, nor is it a simple one. To be a mother demands that a woman takes on a complex identity (Richardson, 1993). She is still herself but she is also a mother, with the incumbent roles, responsibilities and relationships which this entails. The idea of becoming a mother has been part of most women's identities since childhood and although many accept that they did not really know what motherhood was like until they experienced it, the fact of becoming a mother is no surprise in itself.

Why do women become mothers, or at least take the option of becoming a mother so seriously? On an individual level, women recognise their biological capacity to have children and, through socialisation into the female role, come to equate femininity with marriage and motherhood, often seeing women who do not do this as 'inadequate' (Woollett, 1992). Motherhood potentially provides girls/women with entry into womanhood (Woollett, 1987).

> One of the attractions of motherhood is its normative quality. Motherhood is an expected and normal role for all women. To become a mother is to do what women and those around them expect and want them to do. It is to be the same as other women and not stand out as different. In this ideological context, women's decisions about motherhood are not so much about when to have children, but how many to have and increasingly, in which social context to have them. The mandate for motherhood, as it has been called, means that women opt out of motherhood rather than opting into it.
>
> (Woollett, 1987: 1)

Many women believe that they can only achieve adult, feminine status through becoming mothers. Ann Phoenix's (1991) research with teenage mothers supports this view, in that their desire for motherhood as entry to womanhood is not so much a biological desire to become pregnant and nurture a child as an implicit recognition of apparent privilege unavailable to childless women. This system of beliefs is related to the patriarchal idealisation of women as mothers, which is part of women's subordination. The romanticisation of motherhood, and the sets of relationships which accompany it, are dictated by patriarchal power relations. It suits men for women to mother.

The maternal instinct

The motherhood mandate is serviced by the popular and powerful belief system surrounding the notion of a maternal instinct. This 'instinct' is characterised by two desires – to have children, and to care for them (Figes, 1994). However, it has become increasingly clear that this 'instinct' is a socially constructed myth and that many mothers feel able to express their ambivalence both about their children and the role (Lewis, 1995a and b; Parker, 1995).

Penelope wanted to have a baby because:

> It's a fulfilment – a personal fulfilment different from other aspects of fulfilment. It's a very strong biological urge. I can't explain it any other way. I just wanted to have a baby.
>
> (Penelope)

However, Wendy felt differently.

> I've never felt in any way maternal at all. As soon as I found out I was shocked. I was upset, and even up to now [36 weeks into the pregnancy] I can say that … at the moment I just feel fat, and I feel movement inside me, but the thought that it's a person and I've got to be responsible – that I don't think has hit me yet.
>
> (Wendy)

The notion of the maternal instinct underpins the contemporary construction of motherhood. It underlies notions of femininity and required maternal behaviour, and its absence is used to explain women's maternal failures, such as not protecting children from or perpetrating child abuse or neglect. It is also used, in conjunction with theories of attachment, to explain childhood anxieties, subsequent problems in adulthood and in developing childbirth and day-care policies.

The myth of femininity encapsulated by this notion of the maternal instinct is the one through which women's psychology and social role are determined scientifically (Apter, 1993). This myth may be summarised thus:

1 All women have a biological drive towards conceiving and bearing children.
2 This is a precursor to the drive to *nurture* those children.
3 The skills/capacities required to care for infants/children emerge or evolve immediately after the birth without the need for training.

The logical consequence of this instinct would be the knowledge that all women want to (and thus should be enabled to) have children, and are capable of looking after them without training. The maternal instinct cuts across ideas that women are *socialised* into wanting children – it is a biological imperative (Buss, 1994).

Feminist research has challenged such myths by showing contradictions within the idea of a maternal instinct, for example by observing that doctors differentiate between those who possess the maternal instinct (married women) and those who do not (unmarried women). Married women are encouraged to seek fertility counselling if necessary, and condemned for wanting abortions. Unmarried women (especially lesbians; see Burns, 1992) are challenged for wanting children (Boyle, 1992).

There certainly appears to be little historical or psychological evidence for an innate desire either to bear or to nurture children (Parker, 1995). Elisabeth Badinter (1981), for example, distinguished maternal 'instinct' from 'love' in her historically grounded critique of motherhood: 'Maternal love is a human feeling. And like any feelings, it is uncertain, fragile and imperfect. Contrary to many assumptions, it is not a deeply rooted given in women's natures' (Badinter, 1981: xxiii). She provided evidence of historical variations in maternal behaviour which sometimes reflect interest in and devotion to the child, and sometimes not (Riley, 1983). Research on women's responses to their new-born infants further challenges the belief about instinctual maternal love (Crouch and Manderson, 1995), but does identify the influence of the scientific experts' advice, through the fact that women expect to feel this and experience guilt and distress when they do not (Nicolson, 1988).

What is apparent is that when women have children (whether or not the children are planned) they usually try their best to care for them and often grow to love them. Many evaluate their personal worth through this relationship and discharge their responsibilities as well as they are able.

The motherhood role, contrary to the ideology of the maternal instinct, appears to be one for which most women are ill-prepared. However, it is an experience which seems to be reproduced from generation to generation of women, and women continue to mother. Why should this be the case? Nancy Chodorow (1978) has suggested that this reproduction of mothering within the context of patriarchy, although not a biological imperative, is in one sense both natural and inevitable for women, given the dominant social structures. Women's mothering is not only a product of biology, but also causally related to historical conditions and the way that child-care and the division of labour have evolved. She argued that girls/women and boys/men develop in a context which encourages psychological capacities and commitments to participate in the existing social relations and structures. The dominant structures, whereby women mother and men work outside the home, are accompanied by appropriate psychological capacities which underlie these tasks, and these are reproduced at both conscious and unconscious levels:

> Women as mothers produce daughters with mothering capacities and the desire to mother. These capacities and needs are built into and grow out of the mother–daughter relationship itself. By contrast, women as mothers (and men as not-mothers) produce sons whose nurturant capacities and needs have been systematically curtailed and suppressed.
>
> (Chodorow, 1978: 7)

Many radical feminists have challenged this view, proposing that men avoid sharing child-care because they do not want to do it, not because they are incapable of it. Further, by focusing upon the personality dimension, Nancy Chodorow failed to explore social, economic and other psychological aspects of parenting which might be changed to make shared parenting more of a reality (Richardson, 1993). Chodorow's analysis implies a determinism, with an emphasis on childhood socialisation, which potentially enables men themselves to employ the 'excuse' that they have not been brought up to be good at child-care! Child-care is not mysterious or part of early developmental psychology. It is learnt in adulthood, often following childbirth.

Sue Sharpe (1976) had proposed a very different view of how girls choose and learn to mother, and adopt the accompanying behaviour and beliefs associated with being a woman. Her study, which focused on white, Afro-Caribbean and Asian girls living in London, identified ways in which cultural stereotyping was used to represent the typical or ideal characteristics of women and men so that, despite class differences and changes over time, certain fundamental qualities and beliefs are pervasive and represented as feminine or masculine 'natures'.

School, family and the media all act to reinforce these images of the norm which, on the whole, still suggests men have the more socially desirable traits. Sharpe (1994) found twenty years later that traditional female images of wife, mother homemaker are now mixed with more overt sexuality. The cute pretty image of Olivia Newton John has been replaced by the assertive, sexual Madonna. This co-exists with the expansion of masculinity to include a nurturant side (see also Segal, 1990). Seventy-five per cent of the girls in Sue Sharpe's original study had said they would have chosen to be girls, and part of their choice was 'the anticipated joys and satisfactions of becoming wives and mothers and caring for homes and children' (Sharpe, 1976: 206). She suggested that all the girls had been presented with an idealised image of motherhood and many appeared unaware of its oppressive conditions, so that motherhood remains one of the most positive aspects of the feminine role for many girls. Any conflicts between their futures as housewives and mothers and the low social status of this role did not seem to arise. Some clue to this discrepancy might be their perceived potential of life as a worker outside the home. The limited possibilities in employment, particularly for working-class girls and, because of racism, black girls, contrasted with the possible fulfilment, satisfaction and apparent relative freedom and adult status which comes with the housewife/mother role. So, despite the struggles the girls in this study witnessed in their own mothers' lives, the perceived satisfaction from mothering potentially outweighed the lack of satisfaction they saw in paid employment or unemployment.

Twenty years later girls and boys were experiencing severely reduced prospects of employment. However, girls now appear to have a greater set of possibilities beyond the role of wife and mother. Working-class girls frequently move into white-collar clerical and secretarial occupations more easily than previously, and better-educated girls could opt for professional life more acceptably than in the 1970s. This is reinforced by the higher achievements of many girls in school over those of their male contemporaries.

These greater opportunities may result in delaying parenthood, but girls still want to include motherhood in their lives. Hazel Beckett (1986) and Chris Griffin (1989; 1993) both observed the impact of gender socialisation on young women and men. Hazel Beckett suggests that marriage and motherhood were part of almost all her respondents' eventual aims, while Ros Coward (1992) demonstrates middle-class women's ambivalence to the relationship between career and motherhood.

> On one occasion, when the baby was about six months old I was driving along the motorway – fast, because I was late – when I suddenly thought, this is total madness. I don't want to be this far away from home. I don't want to be doing this job. If I'm going to be spending time away from my child, the job has got to matter more to me.
>
> (Coward, 1992: 22)

However, 'The question of motherhood versus career seems, for the majority, to have been stably resolved in the direction of combining them. They seem to have made a unanimous and unconflicted choice to experience occupational involvement, marriage and motherhood' (Beckett, 1986: 47). From this, she argued that female gender identity contains a flexibility that traditional theorists have ignored.

Chris Griffin's (1986) study of young women from a variety of backgrounds leaving school indicates similarly that:

> Marriage and motherhood were seen as distant events which might occur some ten years in the future, but they were also seen as inevitable for most young women. Few financially feasible or socially acceptable alternatives were available, particularly for young working class women
>
> (1986: 181)

This remains the case as Sue Sharpe (1994) and Terri Apter (1993) observe. Women mother, on the whole, because the motherhood parcel is the one most open to them; other ways of life for women are not as well rewarded. Women are often (unless, for example, they are lesbian or single women) made to feel that there must be something wrong with them if they do not choose to be a mother. Men, on the other hand, although encouraged into a particularly well-defined masculine role which precludes 'mothering', remain more able to choose whether, or how far, to involve themselves in child-rearing (Apter, 1993).

The experience of motherhood

> It was a strange stirring, a sense of dissatisfaction, a yearning that women suffered in the middle of the twentieth century in the United States. Each suburban wife struggled with it alone. As she made the beds, shopped for groceries, matched slip cover material, ate peanut butter sandwiches with her children, chauffeured Cub Scouts and Brownies, lay beside her husband at night, she was afraid to ask, even of herself, the silent question: 'is this all?'
>
> (Friedan, 1963: 13)

Motherhood is not about having babies and living happily ever after – but many women may still believe it is. Early sociological studies in the 1960s and 1970s indicated that the mother/housewife role, which was more common and possibly less complicated then, was not the ideal that women had been led to believe awaited them (Friedan, 1963). Gavron's (1966) study suggested that this cuts across social class groups. She found that expectations of marriage and motherhood contradicted the actual experience, which led to confusion surrounding women's roles. This affected her respondents' attitudes to marriage:

> For some wives of both classes marriage was seen as a kind of freedom; yet when it was combined with motherhood it became a kind of prison and they felt their freedom had been restricted before they had really been free at all.
>
> (Gavron, 1966/77: 136)

Ann Oakley (1976) had found a similar pattern of disillusion and suggested that, while marriage and motherhood are seen as potentially providing the greatest life satisfaction for women, in reality they provide disappointment. Before they become mothers, women have a highly romanticised picture of what motherhood is: 'before motherhood is experienced they want more children than they do later' (Oakley, 1976: 189). Motherhood still appears to be perceived by young women as 'more pliable, more mutable than it turns out to be' (Apter, 1993: 55). Despite some high-profile changes in the fatherhood role, in two-parent, heterosexual families, motherhood is tied to the role of the housewife/homemaker (Apter, 1993). This is the case whether or not the woman works and it cuts across social class groupings (Lewis, 1995a and b).

What makes images of marriage and motherhood so appealing while remaining problematic in reality? Each step in women's 'normal' lives – finding a male partner, marriage and having children – increases the disappointment. The more women fulfil their destiny the more pernicious, it seems, is the trap. Why do women appear not to learn the lessons of their foremothers?

It is difficult for us to believe that our biological destiny and instinctual drives lead us to such a confusing end. It is often not until we come face to face with motherhood itself that we realise, through experience, that this idealised image is a patriarchal myth. What is it that causes this confusion? If motherhood is so bad, why do women not just opt out?

To understand this it is necessary to look in more detail at what mothering entails. Some studies have focused upon changes in role and social status following childbirth which demonstrate the reorientation of women's domestic and working lives once they have had a baby (Oakley, 1979); others focus on more psychological dimensions, examining it as a life transition which requires psychological adjustment in identity (Nicolson, 1988; Lewis, 1995a and b). Although arguably a woman's identity as a mother starts in childhood, the process of actually giving birth to and caring for a baby changes most women's sense of themselves and also their values and beliefs. Many women report that it is not until they do become mothers that this change becomes a reality (Nicolson, 1988). The initial transition to motherhood is a shock in a number of ways – physically and emotionally (Oakley, 1980) – and this does not appear to diminish with second or subsequent births. Each time the pressures, hard work and need to relearn child-care skills confronts each woman anew. With each child, women are expected, and expect themselves, to take primary child-care responsibility regardless of their other responsibilities or their specific abilities (Apter, 1993).

The practice of mothering (that is, the day-to-day experience of child-care and associated tasks) can be difficult and may lead to depression and unhappiness (Parker, 1995). However, motherhood is not always a negative, stressful, tiring, depressing experience brought about through an oppressive set of social struc-tures. It can also be an exciting, rewarding and emotionally stimulating one. It is inherent paradoxes such as these that produce what Adrienne Rich has described as 'the suffering of ambivalence: the murderous alternation between bitter resent-ment and raw-edged nerves and blissful gratification and tenderness. Sometimes I seem to myself, in my feelings towards these tiny guiltless beings, a monster of selfishness and intolerance' (Rich, 1984: 21). Rozsiker Parker (1995) has more recently reiterated this: 'Much of the guilt with which mothers are familiar stems from difficulties in weathering the complicated and contradictory feelings pro-voked by maternal ambivalence' (Parker, 1995: 1). It is the children themselves who produce rewards, and the motherhood role includes the power, responsibil-ity, satisfaction and independence that child-rearing brings, as well as the bore-dom, hard work and pain. Motherhood can introduce meaning and purpose into life as well as bring new opportunities for exploring a woman's own capacities, and forming relationships: 'Having children can bring greater vitality, fun and humour into our lives, as well as providing us with a different insight into the world' (Richardson, 1993: 1). Supporting this view, Sian Lewis (1995a and b) found that several mothers reported their children to be rewarding companions, which, provided they were financially secure and emotionally supported by a partner or friends, helped them overcome much of the negative experience of routine child-care.

Motherhood certainly does qualitatively change women's lives, for better and worse. Even so, motherhood remains a low-status role in patriarchal society. Fur-ther, the image of the 'mother', things that mothers do, qualities they are per-ceived to have, their additional strengths and achievements are often treated with a degree of disdain, although this co-exists with the idealised view that mother-hood is the most important job in the world (Figes, 1994).

While there is no evidence that women are innately endowed with special ma-ternal qualities, the experience of mothering does enable women (and men) to develop skills and capacities which can be generalised to other activities. Also, being a mother may stimulate particular ways of perceiving and explaining the world. This is what Sarah Ruddick has called 'maternal thinking' which, she claims, evolves through the very experience of being a mother who of necessity engages in the universal and culturally prescribed practices needed to maintain a child's life and nurture it. Socially and psychologically, mothers develop a distinctive way of seeing and being in the world in order to accomplish this, and mothers frequently adopt a style of humility and cheerfulness to cope with their priority activities. However,

> Because in the dominant society 'humility' and 'cheerfulness' name virtues of subordinates, and because these virtues have in fact developed in conditions of subordination, it is difficult to credit them, and easy to confuse them with self-effacement and cheery denial that are degenerative forms.
>
> (Ruddick, 1982: 81)

In fact, Ruddick argues, far from motherhood being a humble activity, 'maternal thinking' demonstrates resilience and strength. Mothers need to be strong to cope with mothering and with the social conditions surrounding that role: childrearing; running the home; managing complementary child-care arrangements; and maintaining relationships with their partners, family, friends and others. They have to be strong in order to maintain a sense of their own identity and fulfil some of their own needs and negotiate their way through the associated social subordination. A feminist consciousness and feminist analysis of motherhood helps to enable this to happen, and makes women's strengths explicit (Apter, 1993).

Feminism and motherhood: towards the future

> ... the aim of feminism is not to free women from motherhood but from the conditions in which they find motherhood oppressive.
>
> (Richardson, 1993: 124)

Despite the research by sociologists, psychologists and other experts, it has been primarily through the effects of feminist writers that the reality of mothers' lives, and the impact of the idealisation of motherhood and the family upon girls'/women's experience, that the conditions of motherhood have been made explicit.

Feminist writers have paid sustained attention to the experience of being a woman and the ways in which motherhood impinges upon women's lives. Accounts of childbirth prior to the work of Ann Oakley tended to be either medical or to extol the joys and fulfilment of childbirth for the truly feminine woman. Feminist writers, while not denying the pleasures of children and the various experiences of childbirth, explored the medicalisation of birth and the ways in which women's control (both as professionals and mothers) had been eroded (Oakley, 1980; Nicolson, 1988). Recognition of patriarchal control of women's bodies inspired women's action in a number of ways over childbirth, for instance the right to home births and the challenge to routine induced deliveries, fashionable in the mid-1970s.

Understanding the daily lives of mothers with young children was first made explicit by Hannah Gavron (1966), who was followed by other writers who have made further contributions towards explaining the conditions of motherhood (Boulton, 1983; Sharpe, 1994). Gavron specifically explored issues of class and motherhood, and noted the way in which, for both working- and middle-class women, becoming a mother changed their lives as they lost their independence. However, her work also clarified the ways in which social class differences are exacerbated with the transition to motherhood, as social class is, in part, determined through men's levels of income and, as mothers, married and cohabiting women are more likely to be dependent on men.

Almost twenty years later, Mary Boulton's (1983) study supported the view that experiences of motherhood are to some extent class-related. Although all the mothers in her study reported positive and negative aspects of mothering:

> A large house and domestic conveniences ... can lighten the burden of child care and give a woman the time and space for her interests apart from the children; a car and telephone can also help her maintain these interests as well as reduce her sense of isolation at home.
>
> (Boulton, 1983: 205)

For the vast majority of women, these may only be obtained with the help of a partner and even then are clearly subject to social and economic status. Lone mothers, as argued above, are more likely to be poor, in bad housing and less well educated, so for them the oppressive conditions of motherhood remain unalleviated.

The married woman, however, despite the possibility of greater affluence, does not avoid oppression. Just as there were in Friedan (1963), there are still issues about the lack of satisfaction in a woman's relationship with her partner and the sense of pointlessness in her life when she realises she has been pursuing a myth. This myth of marriage and motherhood has been sustained despite some changes in domestic roles. Since the 1970s much attention has been paid to men's fathering. The representations by experts of the benefits to men and their children of being active fathers were discussed earlier, along with the evidence that men's fathering is usually on their own terms. Popular ideas about the fatherhood role have changed so that men are expected to, and expect themselves to, enjoy children. The idea that particularly middle-class men would take an equal part in domestic activities after becoming parents has, however, been challenged by a number of studies.

As Lynne Segal (1990) argues, men will be persuaded to be more involved in fathering when conditions of parenting become more flexible, ensuring maximum choice in terms of child-care, domestic and employment arrangements.

Conclusion

Despite the centrality of motherhood in women's lives, and the contributions of feminist writers to challenging the invisibility of women's own experience as mothers, feminist analysis has had an ambivalent relationship with motherhood. This may be due in part to the overemphasis upon middle-class white heterosexual women which emerged from early work such as Friedan's, and perhaps a failure to understand the covert pressures towards maternity. Perhaps many feminist writers lost patience with the problems faced by 'comfortable' mothers when there were potentially more pressing political issues.

2

COMPETING EXPLANATIONS OF POST-NATAL DEPRESSION

The consequences of perinatal mental disorders are costly, not only in terms of personal suffering, but in their potential for increasing long-term demands on health care services. Depression is not only an unpleasant personal experience but can jeopardise the survival of a family; an infant's emotional and cognitive development may be affected and a 'rejected' and dejected partner may leave home. A desperate mother may decide to end her own life and/or that of her children.

(Cox and Holden, 1994: ix)

Today mothers and children are confined together in small spaces. For many there is no alternative and no relief. Even if facilities exist, such as playgroups or mother and toddler clubs, they necessitate a special expedition which requires planning and preparation. Whole days may go by during which they see only each other and the mother may have no adult contact beyond the check-out girl at the supermarket. There may be no one else in her life who is interested in the baby and no one with whom she can discuss him.

(Dally, 1982: 201)

Introduction

The extracts above demonstrate two contrasting perspectives on the plight of the isolated mother. The focus on the demands a depressed mother makes on healthcare services, families, children and partners tells a different tale from that from the woman's perspective in the second extract. Which of them is most important? How and why do societies, families and individuals appear to collude in the blatant lack of support that both of these pictures depict? Part of the answer lies in the strength of the myth of motherhood as natural, desirable and unequivocally fulfilling for all women. Almost everyone, male and female, subscribes to this to some extent and yet almost everyone fails to achieve fulfilment and success. It seems that, despite the fact that the human race only survives because it reproduces itself, western industrial societies do not have the knowledge or the will to make motherhood a positive experience. This is due to the way knowledge is collected and disseminated. Paradoxically, while scientists portray their knowledge as unbiased and impartial, what they are interested in asking derives from a very clear standpoint. That perspective is at the opposite end of the spectrum from the concerns of mothers.

What we know about becoming a mother therefore varies according to whether we are concerned with scientific knowledge – portrayed as objective and generalisable – or whether the interest is upon how women experience motherhood – seen to be subjective and anecdotal.

Becoming a mother has an impact of the life of the woman, each time it occurs, physically, socially, economically and emotionally. The ways in which motherhood affects each woman also cross over into the lives of her baby, the baby's father, her family and friends. The success of the transition from pregnancy to motherhood has concerned experts and lay people alike. As argued in the previous chapter, there are distinct rules, written and unwritten, that place the burden for the smooth transition to good mothering firmly upon the individual woman. When she fails to adapt to the role of mothering an infant, she is identified as having PND.

The post-natal period is a site of lively interdisciplinary debate. Medical, midwifery, nursing, psychological, social and lay childbirth experts all believe they can contribute to the mother and baby's well-being at this stage. The focus of their attention is about what has gone wrong for a woman if she has become depressed. What causes PND? Who gets it? Can it be predicted? What is its incidence? Will it happen more than once to the same woman? are among questions which have not been answered to the satisfaction of all who have an interest in this area. What is clear, though, is that in the region of eight out of ten women experience some degree of depression and despair during the days and months after the birth of their baby. This leads to additional difficulties in their relationships and in child-care. It also influences the woman's image of herself as a 'good mother'. There seems to be a severe mismatch between the culture that expresses the view that all women make good, natural mothers and the day-to-day reality of looking after a baby.

In this chapter I examine what expert researchers have to say in response to questions about PND and suggest that, despite the increase in research on the subject, available knowledge is represented by competing explanations which do not appear to connect. The extremes are represented by medical accounts, which focus upon the biological explanations, and feminist accounts, which emphasise the inherent difficulties that the traditional social context places upon the lives of mothers. Furthermore, there is interesting evidence that a great many women themselves choose to see any negative post-natal experiences as being linked to their biology rather than the social context. The reasons for this lie in the power of medical discourses, which for over one hundred years, have served to position women as pathological, with irrational, unstable minds, in direct contrast to men, who are sane, rational and reliable.

Images of women and motherhood

Elaine Showalter has described the way in which women's minds were constructed by the developing, exclusively male, nineteenth-century medical profession as weak and out of control following childbirth (Showalter, 1978). This point has also been made by other writers examining the relationship between women and their doctors over the last 150 years (see Ehrenreich and English, 1979; Ussher, 1989; 1991).

The developing science of obstetrics and gynaecology stressed that women, by virtue of their bodies and particularly as a consequence of their hormone functions, were 'pathological specimens of the human race' (Moscucci, 1993: 31). It was women's biology that was seen to govern their bodies and their minds, rendering them the weaker sex.

> The leniency with which women were treated in infanticide cases is one example of how this principle was applied in practice: at times of heightened sexual activity such as childbirth and the puerperium, women became physiologically and psychologically vulnerable and could not be regarded as criminologically responsible for their actions.
>
> (Moscucci, 1993: 31)

From that tradition, and the belief that women were both weak and in need of control, sprang the theoretical and empirical focus which continues to underpin contemporary medical practice: that women's minds and hormones are co-dependent and that the female body and mind are beyond women's personal command (e.g. see Ussher, 1989; Moscucci, 1993).

Thus, PND is still seen by many experts and lay people as distinct both from the social context of childbirth and motherhood and from any other kind of depression. It is frequently described as an irrational, inevitable response to the hormone fluctuations following childbirth. Nevertheless, despite the attention of experts, until 1992 neither the Diagnostic and Statistical Manual of the American Psychiatric Association nor the World Health Organisation identified PND as a distinct diagnosis (Whiffen, 1992; Cox, 1994). Knowledge about PND was based on belief, myth and a body of contentious empirical evidence. However, this did not prevent post-natal depression being, as John Cox asserts,

> ... a diagnostic term regarded by most women as useful, and for this reason alone in a 'user-oriented' service it could be included in a classification, which would then reflect actual usage; most women regard post-natal depression as 'different' from depression at other times.
>
> (Cox, 1994: 5)

But is the fact that women might find the term and diagnosis useful equivalent to taking women's explanations seriously? This is the key feminist contention. Valerie Thurtle (1995) suggests that perhaps women's perceptions *seem* so similar to those of the medical profession because medical explanations are frequently equated to legitimate facts and 'the dominant ideas in the press might encourage them to describe their ideas in these terms' (1995: 417). It seems as if PND has become a 'folk concept' relating to any psychological difficulty after childbirth which might not hold the same meaning for all women or their medical advisors (Thurtle, 1995). Labelling a condition may have a short-term comforting effect whereby the recipient of a diagnosis may feel she is not the only one to suffer in that way, but in the longer term labels do not effect a 'cure'.

So long as mainstream research (and resulting clinical practice) fails to challenge the 'femininity as pathology' myth, the benefit of PND as a concept for understanding and improving women's mental health must remain contentious.

What is post-natal depression?

Popular psychology books embrace post-natal depression as an objective, easily identifiable phenomenon, taking the widespread awareness of this view for granted. For example, as a counterbalance to the myth of 'joyful' motherhood, one such book asserts:

> Since most pregnant women and their families fear that this [postpartum psychosis requiring hospitalisation] will happen to them, it is perhaps a comfort to know that only 0.2% of women are so severely affected. While 80% of new mothers experience some degree of depression or weepiness during the days or weeks after the birth, 10% are somewhere in the middle, suffering a longer period of emotional disturbance, but this is not sufficiently serious to need long-term treatment.
>
> (Blumfield, 1992: 31)

Aetiology and causation are also uncontested in these popular texts:

> Postpartum depression can begin anytime during the first two months of your baby's life. The symptoms of depression are variable; but what distinguishes them from normal adjustment symptoms is that they persist after your baby is six to eight weeks old, and seem to affect you most of the time rather than just some of the time. You may notice extreme changes of appetite – either overeating or under-eating. Changes in sleep patterns are also common – sleeping more, or having broken sleep. Other symptoms include tearfulness and crying spells, a short attention span and problems concentrating, and spells of depression. ... As with other hormone-related syndromes like PMS, you may find yourself increasingly irritable and over-sensitive.
>
> (Dunnewold and Sanford, 1994: 23–4)

In popular accounts, the symptoms and causes of PND are routinely taken to be directly related to the physiology of childbirth, particularly the hormone changes that take place following labour, although sometimes physical exhaustion is acknowledged as playing its part. These explanations, presented so simply and unproblematically, comprise a substantial component of the corpus of knowledge on PND, which has taken on a new lease of life within and between the social and clinical sciences over the past twenty years, specifically gathering momentum in the 1990s. Nevertheless, the answer to the question 'what is post-natal depression?' remains both unclear and unsatisfactory (see for example Whiffen, 1992).

Post-natal depression: the 'scientific' perspective

The research literature on post-natal depression spans the course of a century, although the emphasis and focus has varied from concern with severe psychiatric illness to clinical depression, 'maternity blues' and, most recently, the impact of maternal depression on the family. Between 1980 and 1990 more than one hundred studies on PND were published (Whiffen, 1992).

Despite these increasingly abundant data, it remains difficult to grasp whether there have been any advances in explanations of why women get depressed after childbirth. If PND is caused by hormone changes at the time of birth, why do significant numbers of women *not* get depressed at that stage? Why do some women suffer from psychotic episodes and others not? Are psychological problems following childbirth, from psychosis to mild depression, part of a continuum or a series of different unrelated conditions? Are there any qualitative differences between depression at this time and at other times in a woman's life, or indeed between PND and depression suffered by men?

There are rational reasons why (particularly) medical research has reached this impasse. Contemporary medical research is characterised by large-scale randomised control trials, frequently sponsored by government agencies or multinational drug companies, seeking to identify the effectiveness of one treatment over another (see Oakley, 1990). While not all clinical research is funded this way, the model of the RCT (randomised control trial) is the standard from which other forms of research are seen to *deviate* and have to justify their designs from such as basis. In order to operate within this framework, it is standard practice to take for granted an objective means of identifying an 'illness'. Thus the concept of PND is not seen to be problematic. What counts is that there are effective screening instruments (in this case the EPDS (see Cox and Holden, 1994) is generally accepted to have been validated for this purpose). From that point on, interventions are evaluated (e.g. a randomly selected group of depressed new mothers might be given specialised health visitor support and the outcome compared to that of others who only have the traditional consultation pattern).

Alternative approaches are epidemiological studies using screening instruments and other validated measures to predict the distribution of those who have morbid scores throughout the wider population and to attempt to relate the morbid score to other variables such as age, marital status, social class and so on. There is a lot to be said in favour of these kinds of studies, particularly when specifically physical conditions are being studied. What is difficult to accept in the context of studying PND is the assumption that the screening instrument works in detecting

LIVERPOOL
JOHN MOORES UNIVERSITY
AVRIL ROBARTS LRC
TEL. 0151 231 4022

depression and that the scales within it bear any relation to the experience of being a new mother (this will be discussed in more detail in Chapter 3).

Unsurprisingly, a major characteristic of the currently available traditional research literature is that almost none of the scientific papers set out a clear operational definition of PND. It is assumed that, if a comparable instrument to that used in other studies is employed, then the researchers will be measuring the same thing.

This point has not escaped the critics. Almost twenty years ago, in the early 1980s, commentators argued that the literature has 'failed to distinguish among the maternity blues, post partum affective psychoses, and mild to moderate post partum depression' (Hopkins *et al.*, 1984: 498). And studies of PND 'are beset by methodological problems such as problems in the definition of depression itself' (Pollock *et al.*, 1980: 1). However, despite the absence of operational definitions, an implicit model of PND has emerged. PND is characterised by scientists through its *temporal location*, as occurring during the first twelve months following childbirth; the *variety of its form*, which varies according to when during the post-natal period and how long depressive episodes occur; whether it is in fact an 'illness' with a physical cause, or a *response* to 'stress' or a 'life event'; how far it is actually *linked to childbirth itself* or simply connected to being a new mother; and finally there is interest in the *incidence*.

When does post-natal depression develop?

PND is defined, somewhat tautologically, as depression that occurs during the first twelve months following childbirth. The origin of this 'cut-off' stems from the work of Marcé, a nineteenth-century French psychiatrist who drew attention to the view that 'postpartum illness' was separate in time and type from other psychiatric disorders (see Pitt, 1978). This view has proved compelling in clinical circles, as witnessed by the Marcé Society, established in 1982 and continuing to flourish, for the study of motherhood and mental illness.

Within the time span of twelve post-natal months, however, there is a relative deficiency in the information about duration and course (Hopkins *et al.*, 1984). Some evidence suggests PND lasts from six to eight weeks (O'Hara *et al.*, 1983) whereas other studies suggest that problems may persist throughout the first year (Pitt, 1968; Ballinger *et al.*, 1979). Pollock and colleagues indicate that PND has an influence on the mother for at least three years. Moreover, Brown and Harris (1978) and Lewis (1995a) have shown that women with young children up to school age often report being depressed. Is this PND? What is in question from this evidence is the *clinical* significance of the relationship between *childbirth* and depression.

The symptoms and signs of PND

Whether or not a woman is displaying the signs and symptoms of PND is of primary importance to clinicians from all disciplinary backgrounds. However, these are not always clear from the research literature. The term PND loosely appears to embrace a variety of 'conditions'. Oakley (1979) identified these as (a) the blues, which was a weepiness and anxiety that occurred between two and ten days following the birth which is usually seen to be transitory (Pitt, 1968; Harris, 1981; Kendell *et al.*, 1984; York, 1990); (b) depression and anxiety on arriving home with the baby which lasts a week or two (Cox *et al.*, 1983); (c) depressed 'moods' with good and bad days around three months after delivery (Oakley, 1980); (d) clinical depression which is enduring and includes other symptoms such as loss of appetite and sleep disturbance (Hopkins *et al.*, 1984; Dalton, 1989).

PND, it appears, is used non-specifically as a 'catch-all' diagnosis for emotional and psychiatric problems after childbirth. However, the variety of the forms of depression it covers seems to be very different in its manifestations and thus probably causation. Most of the researchers seem to put effort into distinguishing between PND and other forms of depression (see Littlewood and McHugh 1997, quoting Dalton, 1980) rather than trying to see whether different kinds of depression occur following childbirth (Green, 1998).

Is PND an 'illness' or a logical response to 'stress'?

What causes PND? Is it the biology of childbirth or is it the stress of labour, breast-feeding and looking after a baby? Characteristic of much traditional research on post-natal depression is that it is unproblematically perceived as a psychiatric condition. Despite almost thirty years of research there is still a lack of clarity about the similarities and differences between post-natal mental illness, depression and psychosis. Several authors who set out to describe one kind of 'disorder' (as listed in the section above) are prone to 'concept slippage', thereby referring to a broadly located 'post-partum mental illness' or 'psychiatric disorders associated with childbearing' (e.g. Margison, 1990). Moreover, this conceptual framework is used time and again to embrace 'conditions' that are not taken to be psychiatric in any practical sense, and are not typically referred for psychiatric treatment.

The debate concerning the relationship between puerperal psychosis and other post-partum 'disorders' – whether they are mutually exclusive or form part of a continuum – has not been resolved either (Sneddon, 1982). Neither has the debate on how far, if at all, post-natal 'illnesses' differ qualitatively from non-puerperal conditions (Katona, 1982). As Appleby asserts: 'Little progress has been made towards an understanding of the aetiology of postpartum psychosis, despite the long-standing assumption that it is precipitated by biological factors' (Appleby, 1990: 109).

Researchers interested in PND as a response to childbirth as a life event focus on depression as a reaction to stress and the lack of social support (Oakley, 1980; Elliot, 1990) and on the whole tend to be social scientists rather than medically oriented researchers. However, since the mid-1980s there has been more tolerance among the latter group towards recognising depression as a *rational* reaction to stress, thus taking childbirth and other aspects of early motherhood as generally militating against maternal well-being.

Is PND linked to childbirth?

Childbirth is an exciting event. Hormone fluctuations during the latter part of pregnancy are brought to a dramatic conclusion following birth and with the beginning of lactation. Also, labour is tiring, painful and potentially frightening as well as exciting. Childbirth often involves intervention, for example by Caesarean, an epidural to aid a forceps delivery or an episiotomy. All of these have physical and emotional consequences. It would be surprising, then, if such an experience did not have repercussions. However, the traditional research which explores the relationship between PND and birth makes the focus of study the physiology of the event rather than the physical and emotional context.

Despite the adherence to the 'Marcé model' which asserts this link, the literature is pervaded by undercurrents of doubt. Brockington and Kumar (1982) suggested that the 'precise' definition of the links between motherhood and mental illness is 'elusive', which potentially raises doubts about the special and unique relationship (Brockington and Kumar, 1982: 2). They declare, though, that they themselves are convinced of the link – although they are going with their instincts rather than the evidence.

Steiner (1979), reviewing the psychobiology of mental disorders associated with childbearing, argued that:

> Postpartum mental illness is not a unitary phenomenon. The physiology of the puerperium is thus not a cause in itself of any of the symptoms, but rather must be regarded as a contributing or triggering factor acting upon an underlying pre-disposition.
>
> (Steiner, 1979: 449)

In other words, there is little evidence that the biology of childbirth or breast-feeding *per se* precipitates mental illness. Therefore clinical problems that occur during this period are either triggered by non-biological factors or are attributable to other causes.

Cox (1994) found that it was not until 1992 that the World Health Organisation accorded puerperal mental disorders the status of a separate category.

> The new version of their International Classification of Diseases (ICD-10; WHO, 1992) does, however, go some way towards addressing this issue. Mental disorders occurring at this time may now be categorised as puerperal, but only if they cannot otherwise be classified.
>
> (Cox, 1994: 4)

Why, then, do scientists continue to portray the link between motherhood and mental illness as incontrovertible? Why is depression in new mothers not simply seen to be the logical result of stress, exhaustion, learning new skills, and adapting to the imposition of new patterns of relationships and family routines? (This will be discussed further in Chapter 3).

Incidence of PND

There is little consensus on the incidence of PND (Hopkins *et al.*, 1984). There are claims that 7% (Dalton, 1971), between 10 and 20% (York, 1990), 24% (Frate *et al.*, 1979), and 30% (Gordon *et al.*, 1965) of women have depression severe enough to need treatment; 50–80% experience the 'blues' (Pitt, 1968; Harris, 1981; York, 1990) and 33% experience depressed moods (Oakley, 1979).

Hopkins and colleagues (1984) argue that these disparities are due to the lack of comparable criteria for measurement. Oates (1994) indicates that it is also likely that many 'cases' lie undetected.

Competing models of PND

The literature on post-natal depression divides roughly into two approaches or models: 'medical' and 'social science' models, where the former emphasises individual characteristics that *predispose women to becoming depressed* after childbirth and the latter stresses external, *psychosocial factors which act as stressors*.

These positions are to an extent reflected in my respondents' beliefs about themselves (see also Chapters 5 and 6). Some saw themselves as being predisposed to depression, albeit with qualifications. The majority, however, despite having had episodes of depression in the past, saw their emotional state following the birth as complex, usually connected with tiredness and stress rather than individual predisposition.

The medical perspective

Discussion of problematic histories or congenital vulnerabilities overlaps with the debate about the unity of PND (Barzilai and Davies, 1973). Further, some researchers argue that depression at any stage of the life cycle is due to hormonal imbalances and attempts have been made to link post-natal depression and premenstrual tension (e.g. Anzalone, 1977; Dalton, 1971). Dalton goes so far as to argue that PND will either cease or become more moderate once menstruation recurs (Dalton, 1980).

Some studies have proposed that an episode of the 'blues' predisposes women to subsequent PND (e.g. Paykel *et al.*, 1980; Cox *et al.*, 1982), although Kumar and Robson (1978) did not find this link. Cox *et al.* (1982) suggest: 'The blues are not correctly described ... as either trivial or fleeting, and may ... be an important predictor of women at risk of developing a depressive illness later on' (Cox *et al.*, 1982: 115). However, at three months post-partum in another study Cox found 'a further 15% of women had less continuous depressive episodes which were nevertheless totally distinct from the postnatal blues' (Cox *et al.*, 1982: 1). Holden (1994) argues that PND may be the precursor for depression later in life. Others have linked anxiety and depression in pregnancy to PND (Tod, 1964; Dalton, 1971), although Cox *et al.* (1982) could not confirm that women free of symptoms during pregnancy could become depressed post-natally. Davidson (1972) and Pitt (1973) have linked ambivalent and hostile feelings in early pregnancy with the 'blues'. Frommer and O'Shea (1973) have also linked attitudes towards pregnancy and subsequent depression. A family history of emotional disorder has also been connected to PND (Nilsson, 1970; Gordon *et al.*, 1965; Ballinger *et al.*, 1979).

The social science perspective

Social scientists take more account of the context of early motherhood and the experience of birth in order to develop their theoretical positions. Hopkins *et al.* (1984) see research on post-partum depression as offering a 'unique opportunity to clarify the relationship between a specific stressor (the birth of a child) and the development of psychiatric illness' (Hopkins *et al.*, 1984: 498). They are persuaded by evidence suggesting that stressful life events are a significant influence in the development of depression (Brown and Harris, 1978) and that because childbirth is a significant stressor in its own right additional stresses in this period contribute towards depression. This concurs with the early findings of Sandra Elliot (1985), who further proposed that 'Post-natal depression is ... a realistic response to the life event of birth and to the stress of the maternal role, in combination with other life stresses' (Elliot, 1985: 3). The stressors documented include unsatisfactory marriages (Kumar and Robson, 1978; Paykel *et al.*, 1980; Cox *et al.*, 1982; Rossan, 1987), loneliness and lack of adult company (Sharpe, 1994), as well as the role changes that might be involved for some women during the transition to motherhood such as leaving paid employment, running a home and taking responsibility for infant care (Elliot, 1985). Further, lack of social support has been documented as leading to depression (Henderson, 1981; Mueller, 1980), although it is only a few studies (O'Hara *et al.*, 1983; Paykel *et al.*, 1980) that have related social support specifically to PND, until recently.

Hopkins and colleagues (1984) argued that cause and effect in relation to stressors and PND had not been explored effectively. However, much effort has gone into investigating the relationship between childbirth as a life event since the mid-1980s and there is evidence that depression can be alleviated through the provision of practical and social support (Elliot, 1990). However:

> Depression was found to be associated with psychosocial variables. Yet when divided into subgroups according to clinical case histories, a few women fell into a category of depression not explained by current circumstances or relevant previous events. It was suggested that these might therefore be open to explanations in terms of birth related physical changes.

> (Elliot, 1990: 147)

Finally, there is evidence that an unsatisfactory birth experience may be related to subsequent depression, either because of technological intervention (Oakley,

1980; Day, 1982), including induction, or because of poor quality medical care, suggesting that women are more prepared to endure pain than to lose control over labour and delivery (Cartwright, 1979). Tew (1978) and Kitzinger (1978) both argue that hospital rather than home births are more likely to make women depressed.

Implicit in the literature taking the 'medical' position is that a woman who has a baby does not 'normally' experience negative emotions. If she cannot cope or feels depressed it is her fault. She is perceived as being pathological and her reaction one which may require treatment.

The 'social science' position embraces a more liberal, broader view of the individual in context, conceptualising her as a potential victim of social stress. Although this model proposes the view that PND is an understandable reaction to stress, it fails to identify how the *experience itself* varies between individuals. Through focusing upon the general impact of stressors on the potentially vulnerable, it fails to take account of the *meaning* of each event in the individual's life and the potential variation in each woman's experience of becoming a mother and the associated emotions.

Women's experiences of post-natal depression: differing from the experts?

> Conceptions of the human life cycle represent attempts to order and make coherent the unfolding experiences and perceptions, the changing wishes and realities of everyday life. But the nature of such conceptions depends in part on the position of the observer … when the observer is a woman, the perspective may be of a different sort.
>
> (Gilligan, 1993: 5)

Since the mid-1970s[1] feminist psychologists in the USA and Europe have identified the clear influence of gender-bias, in favour of a male perspective, on psychological research and knowledge (Bem, 1993), refocusing attention upon the role of science in constructing a knowledge base that makes women and female perspectives invisible (e.g. Crawford and Maracek, 1989; Wilkinson, 1996). As Gilligan makes clear (see above), it does not matter how reliable scientists believe that their methodology is, in the last resort they interpret their findings through their own, gendered eyes. A man (and most scientists are either men or are involved in teams where a man is the leader) exploring data on PND will see it as a discrete episode in the mother's life which is irrational and related in some way to the biology of birth. There has been a long tradition in which this view has taken shape (see Ehrenreich and English, 1979; Ussher, 1989; Nicolson, 1992a; Moscucci, 1993). The acknowledgement that lack of social support and the stress of early motherhood

---

1 There has been a feminist presence in psychology almost as long as there has been such an academic discipline, but the impetus for a co-ordinated feminist scholarship in the USA and UK arguably dates from the mid-1970s.

are important has only recently been taken seriously but, as argued above, this has been treated simply as a means of *adding* the social context to the biology and does not represent a feminist perspective in which women's experiences are the focal point. For example, it is easy to see that lack of support makes mothering even harder to accomplish and adds to any stress, but this view of lack of support as contributing to an 'illness' is still based on the assumption that *all* women *naturally* make *good* mothers. These good mothers put the needs of their infant and (possibly) other children above their own and not only should they *meet* all their infant's demands, but good mothers should *make* no demands on their children or the baby's father (if he should be present). Good mothers should also take primary responsibility for child-care in the family. Why should all women be perceived in such a homogeneous way? Women are not all the same and their abilities, needs and aptitudes vary. If universal expectations were applied to all men, it would be considered ludicrous. There is no notion in the literature on PND that women have different capacities, desires, needs and lives from each other and that this will inevitably be reflected in the ways they cope with childbirth and early motherhood.

Women talking about post-natal depression implicitly make connections between the fact that the infant enters their lives in a dynamic, developing context and that there is no consistent or objective experience of 'becoming a mother'. They apply this to different occasions when they have had children and to differences between themselves and other women. Each woman implicitly holds her own model to explain her emotional state after childbirth (see Chapters 6 and 7 in particular).

The women I interviewed here described their post-natal emotions and moods intertwined with their own theories of causation, which they frequently located in the changes that the new baby had forced upon their lives.

So for the professional woman:

> All of a sudden you're forced back to being with women. Having been out and feeling free and confident, all of a sudden I was pushed back into a woman's position. I didn't like it. I just couldn't cope.
>
> (Hilary)

> I've done everything in the house I could be bothered to do. I really want to be back at work.
>
> (Felicity)

For some others:

> ... the days drift through in a sense of half washing up, popping round to Sharon's for tea, and I don't know where the days have gone. By the end of the week I've achieved nothing.
>
> (Sylvia)

... and I forget everything and have to write it down – literally from one room to the next.

(Frances)

Just the sheer tiredness. It was just feed, nappy, feed, nappy. I've been absolutely exhausted.

(Lynn)

Whatever the extent of their negative feelings, which sometimes extended to prolonged despair, rarely did my respondents believe their experience was representative of a discrete 'condition' or illness. To them it was complex, distressing, anxiety-provoking and even unpredictable, but essentially part of their own lives.

Conclusions

The scientific understanding of PND has developed over the last twenty years by means of explanations of how often and under what circumstances some women experience it. However, the diverse explanations that remain current in the scientific literature make few concessions to understanding women's own accounts of why they feel as they do. What is missing, it seems, is a means and willingness to explore the complexities in the lives of the women when they have babies. The transition to motherhood can never be a standardised event, because everyone's life is different. Nevertheless, researchers in this area appear daunted by the challenge of explaining PND in its everyday context.

3

THE CONTEXT OF
POST-NATAL DEPRESSION

Introduction

PND, whatever its cause or consequences, occurs within the context of a woman's life: that life does not stop because she has had a baby. Nor is that life directly comparable to that of the woman in the next delivery suite, or the woman at the other end of the country who has had a baby at the same time. Nor are the lives of any of the women in *my* study directly comparable. More important, nor are the lives of women in the studies which have been designed to control for confounding variables such as parity, age, marital status, type of delivery, sex of child or social class by any means identical. Each baby is born into a dynamic social scenario which is both constantly changing and linked through the biographies of the mother and other family members. It is this sense of individuality played out in a gendered, patriarchal context that needs to be understood before any effective understanding of PND can be developed.

In this chapter I explore further the ways in which PND has been explained by traditional researchers and develop a theoretical framework for an explanation of PND which takes women's lives as its central feature.

Ann Oakley (1979) proposed long ago that 'Post-natal depression is not a "scientific" term, but an ideological one. It mystifies the real social and medical factors that lead to mothers' unhappiness' (Oakley, 1979: 12). Her plea was that women's reactions following childbirth should not be seen as pathological but should be explored in their own terms and within the context in which the mothers were leading their lives. Women's experiences of post-natal unhappiness are not symptomatic of individual maladjustment or dysfunction (whether connected with psychological predisposition, hormones or lack of appropriate support networks). There are sensible reasons for women's post-natal distress and labelling it 'illness' does not help.

Through maintaining the model of PND as illness or individual pathology, women's lives remain invisible. What happens to women at home with babies? What is it like to be a full-time mother and housewife rather than being in employment? What is it like to have health-care professionals who are experts on how you should care for and raise your child telling you what to do? What is it like to have problems breast-feeding when you are alone at home with older children and a husband to care for?

Individual circumstances and the social conditions surrounding all motherhood conspire potentially to make mothering a monumental burden, while the social myth persuades us all that motherhood results in happiness. Typical images of motherhood revolve around its being a major source of female self-expression and satisfaction; rarely do women picture themselves in advance as selflessly giving, ignoring their own needs and desires and experiencing loneliness and isolation (Kaplan, 1992; Lewis, 1995b). To subscribe to this dominant myth means that the early days and months of motherhood have a double impact. The inevitable stress, exhaustion, the burden of child-care are set against each woman's fear that she is somehow 'doing it wrong'. Her experience does not relate to her dream.

It is no surprise, then, when some women and families 'buy into' the ideology of PND. Esther Rantzen (1982) publicly upheld the view that depression after childbirth is a clinical condition, declaring herself to be a victim and attempting to offer support to others so that they should not feel any shame or take the blame for being unhappy. Other writers have argued that women suffered *until* PND was taken seriously (Littlewood and McHugh, 1997).

Thus the perspective of those who firmly take the view that the female body is perpetually at risk of PND has been guarded by women who have been distressed after childbirth, and if it appears that women accept this view of their biology and psychology then it is seen as disrespectful to argue against it.

This has become the case with the work of Katherina Dalton, a doctor specialising in HRT for a number of 'female maladies'. She wrote in 1980 that:

> The majority of women suffering from post natal depression do not even recognise they are ill. They believe they are bogged down by utter exhaustion and irritability. It is all too easy to blame their condition on to the extra work the baby brings to their new life. ... Once the condition has been recognised and treated the husband will be able to declare 'She's once more the woman I married.'
>
> (Dalton, 1980: 4)

This is a remarkable position to take up. Women don't have permission to feel low or depressed here *just* because they are exhausted and disillusioned with the conditions of motherhood. They are expected to suffer from a recognised 'illness' before they are permitted to have their behaviour 'excused'. Questions about why it is the *woman* who has to be bogged down by the extra work of having a baby in the family; why the woman, having gone through such a major change in becoming a mother, should in any way be expected to resemble the 'woman he married'; and the defining relation between cause and outcome of such an 'illness' remain unanswered.

Recent assertions about women's experiences of PND suggest that contemporary thinking has not moved in the direction Ann Oakley would have liked.

> Although recent research suggests that the symptoms and duration of post natal depression are not noticeably different from that occurring at other times, depression after having a baby is unarguably unusual in that its effects are experienced at a time when exceptional physical and emotional demands are being made on the mother in caring for her infant and family.
>
> (Holden, 1994: 54)

This extract is revealing in that it reaffirms the view that physical and emotional demands made on the mother during the post-natal period are likely to exacerbate depression, but that somehow this is not relevant to either scientists or clinicians in their endeavours towards understanding and helping these mothers.

Does Holden believe that women are so adept at dealing with their own and others' lives that only unusual women fall prey to depression under these extreme circumstances? Or is it that somehow women's bodies and psychology *per se* render them different from those of men? Are women more volatile, vulnerable and thereby pathological? The intention of the extract above is no doubt compassionate: to lead to the conclusion that detection and treatment of PND is important *for the sake of the woman, her baby and the family* (see Holden, 1994: 55). However, the overall impact on the mythology, science and experience of PND is to marginalise and exclude women from having their experiences taken seriously as mature reactions to adverse and stressful circumstances. Labelling a woman's discerning and carefully thought about responses to the context of their lives as 'illness' affirms women's oppression and their place within the discourse of the 'natural' good mother.

Jeffrey Pearson argued over twenty years ago that the language of illness (e.g. 'symptom', 'illness', 'cure') was the means by which deviant behaviour was identified and controlled under a liberal guise. These words and the ideas and the behaviour behind them were not value-free but loaded in favour of those with power who were in the position of identifying deviants:

> If deviance and social problems can be wound up in this neutral, scientific rhetoric, then uneasy consciences can be put to sleep: action taken against the misfit, which might in any other light appear morally ambiguous, is beyond all moral ambiguity when it is called 'treatment' or 'therapy'.
>
> (Pearson, 1975: 15)

This view is currently seen as old-fashioned. It had been part of an anti-social work, anti-psychiatry movement in the late 1960s and early 1970s that eventually proved limited in its practical application. The past twenty years have seen a change in attitude towards therapy and medicine, which are widely perceived as apolitical and helpful to the individual rather than oppressive; but with these changes a critical edge has also disappeared.

Methodological critique: towards a new paradigm?

The debate between researchers opting for the medical model, versus those choosing a psychosocial model to explain PND, dominates the landscape – there seems no place for other approaches. These researchers focus upon the measurement of PND as an objective, observable and discrete phenomenon and thus by definition the complexities and subjectivity which surround women's experiences of motherhood are disguised (see Nicolson, 1988).

Why should this matter? There is no doubt that developments in mainstream research have ensured a higher public profile for PND, and although the myth of the perfect mother and baby has not been scotched, women on the whole know that motherhood is more difficult than they might otherwise have believed. Large-scale research studies have made a contribution to understanding some important aspects of early motherhood – that many women do get depressed, that this may relate to previous psychological history, that it may bear some relation to hormone changes, tiredness, stress and the lack of social support. Depression has become legitimate in the post-natal period.

Large-scale studies using objective, standardised measures have indeed made important inroads into this area and have been particularly important in challenging the attitudes of some clinicians like Dalton who take an individual pathology model as the standard explanation. It has also been very important to quantify women's experiences. Nevertheless, it needs to be recognised by all involved in the research enterprise, from mainstream medical academics to critical feminists, that both quantitative and qualitative research have important questions to address (see Oakley, 1990). The limits of quantitative research of the type discussed in the previous chapter are the point at which qualitative research can take over.

Large-scale quantitative studies conflate the complexities of women's lives in the post-natal period and the overall message is that some women are depressed and others are not. These kinds of studies by definition do not look at what that experience means to each woman in the context of her life – they focus on variables which may correlate to or potentially even precipitate PND.

Also, by focusing upon collecting data at one point, or several points, along the way during the transition to motherhood, biology or the 'fact of having a baby' is given priority over other things that might be happening – such as a family bereavement, or other life events that are significant to the woman at the time. In other words, it may be that having a baby is not the most important issue influencing well-being during the time of the study, but by fulfilling the study criteria in that parity, age, and so on are compatible with the research needs then it is the physical act of childbirth that is the contingent variable.

A new wave of research that is edging its way to the foreground, such as my study described in this book, takes on board the complexities of women's lives. PND is far more than a 'reaction' to childbirth and early motherhood. It marks the way an individual makes sense of and copes with the circumstances surrounding motherhood – not just those which are directly connected to being a mother, but the things that are happening in her life at that time and how the total circumstances shape her view of what the future might have in store. Taking this more elaborate scenario as the source of data has been supported by practitioners such as midwives and clinical psychologists as being relevant to their understanding of the lives of the women they meet in their everyday work.

Thus, in what follows I suggest an alternative methodology and conceptualisation from that employed in most of the best known studies on PND and develop a rationale for looking beneath the surface to explore the interconnection between biographical context, social support, meaning and experience.

Moving on

This justification for the methods I eventually employed were developed slowly, as my research questions moved away from the traditional ones I had originally set.

In the pilot studies preceding my Ph.D. I used in-depth interviews, a standardised measure of atypical depression following childbirth (Pitt, 1968) and observation with the aim of developing a measure of PND which would control for intervening variables such as personal ill health, other life events, the health of the baby, psychiatric/psychological histories and so on.

In this phase of the research I interviewed forty women from two maternity units in hospital between two and ten days following delivery and at home between ten and twelve weeks later (Nicolson, 1986; 1988). The women were frank and open about their feelings, especially at the second interview.

I categorised the women into those who had high or low scores on the measure at first and second interview. Women with morbid scores at the first interview (the 'blues' period) explained themselves as having negative feelings about their treatment in hospital. These included insensitive staff, poor ward atmosphere, questions not answered, lack of nappies, too few midwives, a bad birth experience, exhaustion, pain and ill-health, anxiety about the baby's health and racism.

Those women who achieved low scores at this stage tended to be satisfied with the care and had few problems with feeding or with their own and the baby's health. High scores at the second interview, however, were founded on a broader base, including social isolation and problems with health.

What was particularly important here, though, was the extent to which the Pitt scores offset what the women actually said about themselves against my observations, particularly of the non-verbal cues. Some women would apparently 'contradict' their answers on the measure, which not only raised issues about validity but, more importantly for what follows, clarified for me that it was important to consider meaning and the relevance of criteria used in validation. So for women who said they were in pain and had sore nipples but responded to the question 'Do you feel you are in good health?' with 'Yes', it seemed essential to find out what they *meant* and *expected* by the term 'good health' at this stage of their lives.

There also appeared to be a tension between 'polite' answers to the formal questions and more detailed answers, often emphasising problems which were only acknowledged when I was not using the questionnaire as a checklist (see Nicolson, 1986; 1988 for a full discussion).

Finally, there were some inconsistencies between people's words, behaviours and the questionnaire answers that were only revealed by observation of non-verbal cues. For example, one woman described herself as happy, but her words and manner suggested this was not the full picture. 'What you would expect with duties towards a man and a family' and 'what you have to do' were phrases that did not sit neatly with happiness in my mind. She did not mention pleasure, nor did she smile at the baby, but talked in a 'tight' way (see Nicolson, 1986; 1988).

From theory to method

The research reported in this book emerged from collection and analysis of in-depth interviews with women over the course of the transition to motherhood. It was analysed to take account of the way they described the experience of the events and the way they placed this transition to motherhood in the context of their own lives. The overall aim of the study was to establish whether there was an objective measurable phenomenon which could be identified as post-natal depression. I also wanted to understand the subjective processes at work in the ways individual women accounted for physical and emotional experiences and to reiterate these within a social context where motherhood has a meaning.

I wanted to see how far women who did experience some depression following childbirth identified any characteristics of their own experience which could be linked to those described by other women in the study. Were there indeed any common features of PND related to the birth *per se* rather than the woman's life and the meaning she placed upon that particular period of time? To what extent is any experience of depression in the post-natal period a reasonable response to specific stresses and pressures?

The design of the research constructed here to answer the research problems stated above was intended to be feminist, qualitative and to operationalise depression from a critical perspective (see Appendix II for details).

Feminism and post-natal depression

The theme of women's biological inferiority has been both implicit and explicit in biological science since the time of Aristotle. It is ... an essential theme for the ideology and cultural practices of society that require women's subordinance both in the home, as homemakers and mothers, and in the marketplace, as underpaid workers in the nurturing, helping and domestic professions.

(Bleier, 1984: vii)

Post-natal depression by definition only happens to women.[1] Since this research was first undertaken in the 1980s, the issues relating to women's reproductive health, feminism and science have become more effectively described than they were then (Ussher, 1989; Nicolson and Ussher, 1992), with a clearer understanding about the relationship between medical science, clinical practice and beliefs about the vulnerability of the female body and mind (Ussher, 1992).

Medical knowledge and practice frame the discourses through which health and ill-health are explained, and the relationships between the values of a profession that discriminates against women and the way that knowledge-claims about women's health are made are intrinsically linked (see Nicolson, 1992b). Women are portrayed frequently as not being fit for 'normal' life, victim to their raging hormones and uncontrollable bodies (Ussher, 1989). Illnesses such as post-natal depression (Nicolson, 1988), the pre-menstrual syndrome (Ussher, 1989) and the menopause (Gannon, 1994) are all to an extent artefacts of patriarchy – both in the identification of the causes of distress, and the classification, explanations and treatments offered (Ussher, 1989). It is not only 'sick' women's bodies that are at the mercy of patriarchy. Women's bodies and psychological experiences have been widely pathologised by the medical profession and associated researchers (Nicolson, 1992a and b; Ussher, 1992).

> The female body is at the centre of the discourse which determines and controls women. To speak of woman is to speak of the body, as femininity has been located within the body, and is constructed by the body. And this is a physical, sexual, fertile body, which houses women's danger, women's power and women's weakness. We, as women, do not own this body, for it has been taken away from us by the phallocentric discourse which represents women and 'the other', as the 'not-I', as somehow lacking – as the second sex. Caught in the gaze of men, the body (and thus the woman) has become the object not the subject.
>
> (Ussher, 1992: 31)

Those women not identified as ill are portrayed as *deficient or dangerous*. Female sexuality, as Jane Ussher suggests above, is traditionally seen as menacing to men. Women as temptresses cause men to lose control over themselves.

Women are also imperfect as well as dangerous because of their hormonal cycles. This perspective on female psychology and physiology remains steadfast in medical and psychological scientific ideas despite evidence of cyclical variations in the performance of males, and the consistent lack of significant outcome measures to demonstrate women's inadequacy at any phases of the cycle (Richardson, 1992).

Women are weak if they are feminine, and culpable if they are not. They are treated by the medical profession as beyond both medical understanding (though

---

1 Some research has been directed towards the father's perspective, but male reaction to parenthood has not been deemed in any way a clinical/pathological condition.

subject to medical knowledge) and control. Evidence for this contradictory position abounds in the clinical and research literature on female aspects of biological reproduction (Ussher, 1989; Nicolson and Ussher, 1992) and mental health (Ussher, 1992). Feminist research in this area takes account of the way women are both portrayed and investigated by scientists through taking issue with the evidence and methodologies.

Qualitative research and women's experience

Psychology, in its attempt to be the science of behaviour, has been desperate to find terms which are impersonal. It has sought to be an animate version of a 'proper science' like chemistry or Newtonian mechanics.

(Gillett, 1995: 111)

Psychology, with its emphasis on *positivistic* scientific methods of research, has been able to develop the means of prediction and to generate behavioural laws similar to those of the physical sciences. However, as Gillett indicates, there is an inherent contradiction in the notion that psychological research (the *science* of behaviour) should emphasise the *impersonal*, while psychologists and other health professionals whose work is informed by psychological knowledge are dealing exclusively with the *personal and interpersonal*. Moreover, the views and experience of the 'subjects' of psychological research are rarely represented.[2] The current resurgence of interest in qualitative methods of research within British psychology (Henwood and Nicolson, 1995) has renewed the debate about the nature of psychology and its status as a science (Harré and Gillett, 1994). Many academics and practitioners who use psychological research to inform their work may be influenced by such contention, perhaps looking on the research evidence derived from qualitative, smaller-scale enquiry as less valid or reliable than survey or experimental data that claim generalisability (Rose, 1985).

Many academics and researchers, however, tend to forget that the social sciences, including psychology, have always been able to draw on a qualitative tradition[3] and reasons for abandoning qualitative research have been more to do with the expediency of experimentation in the process of knowledge accumulation rather than lack of rigour in qualitative psychology (see Nicolson, 1995a).

Mary Boyle (1997) argues that, to be feminist, psychology has to make gender and women's lives visible, and be unequivocally *for* women. However, this

---

2 It is no coincidence that some mothers who have read papers I have published on post-natal depression have taken the trouble to write to me to comment that my work represented one of the few accounts that they could relate to their own experience.

3 For example, Allport who examined life histories from diaries and interviews in 1942. Also William James, the founding father of the discipline, considered that to understand the self a qualitative and self-reflexive approach was necessary.

should not be achieved merely through identifying women solely as the victims of patriarchy. Women experience subordination in a number of ways throughout their lives, and their needs are clearly at odds with the aims, practice and rhetoric of mainstream academic psychology, which seeks to establish norms for human behaviour based upon the white, middle-class bourgeois male (see Sampson, 1993). The problem for feminist psychology is how to represent women's experience of subordination without adding to their burden of misrepresentation (see Tunaley, 1995).

Qualitative research, if conducted well, is as rigorous as quantitative psychology,[4] and the co-existence of both qualitative and quantitative approaches to research is more likely to enhance understanding of the issues being investigated than hinder them.

Following Harré and colleagues (1985), contemporary psychology makes the assumptions that 'each person is a psychological unit in which all important processes occur' (1985: 2). Therefore 'causes' and 'consequences' of individual development are somehow predictable and observable in the individual. Thus, thinking, emotion and gender identity for each of us is taken to be the legacy of our biology and social context, circumscribed within the boundary of the physical body.

Psychology's apparent unquestioning assumption of individualism has not eluded dispute from a number of sources within and outside the discipline (e.g. Harré and Gillett, 1994; Changing the Subject Collective, 1984; Potter and Wetherell, 1987). Neither has the priority given to men and male behaviour as the norm escaped challenge (Henwood and Pidgeon, 1995; Reinhartz, 1985). However, response to these challenges has not led to significant shifts in approach to substance or method in psychology.

Feminist influence in social science has inspired like-minded psychologists, aware that their own discipline has sadly lagged behind sociology, anthropology, human geography and social history (Wilkinson, 1986). Feminist psychologists draw upon feminist theories and methods which overall have been critical of positivism, particularly its requirements for the measurement of observable behaviour and the experimental approach (Reinhartz, 1985), the focus on the unitary subject as the locus of study (Hollway, 1989), and the reliance on male-defined norms as the basis for what counts as knowledge (Ussher, 1989).

Over the past ten years in particular, feminist and social psychologists have begun to take qualitative approaches to research seriously. While there is no intrinsic reason why qualitative research is more feminist than quantitative research (indeed, Celia Kitzinger (1990) has argued that qualitative approaches have been used to pathologise lesbians), the persuasive case has been made for qualitative

---

4 It does need to be considered, however, that the emphasis within the positivist paradigm on 'objectivity' may in itself be problematic, both in terms of the nature of its investigation of human behaviour and in terms of definitions of what science really should be about.

research as conducive to developing knowledge that takes account of the contradictions and conflicts in women's lives (Stanley and Wise, 1983; Wilkinson, 1986; Lewis, 1995b; Tunaley, 1995).

Approaches to qualitative research

One influential development for academic feminists in psychology has been discourse analysis, which is a technique of data collection and analysis with its roots in post-modern critiques of science and knowledge. It prioritises *language and power* as central to all areas of life, and to cultural reproduction. This technique has been explained and operationalised to examine key feminist issues.

It is easy to see how such an approach is valuable to feminists. Post-modern critiques and applications of discourse analysis enable the identification of linguistic repertoires and exposure of structural power relations under patriarchy (Wetherell, 1986). Also, an emphasis on language and power in discourse accounts for the continuity and contradictions in human interactions and emotion (Weedon, 1987). In the process of deconstructing the 'subject-as-agent and the unitary individual ... it provides a critique which gets underneath what is taken for granted by those terms' (Holloway, 1989: 31).

It is also significant to see how some feminists have found this approach to gender power relations to be unacceptable. This is in part because it is potentially 'marginalising' for those who fail to accept the deconstructionist orthodoxy, but more important because of the possibility of depoliticisation in the conceptualisation and reification/celebration of sexual difference.

Searching for self, meaning and experience

While the impact of post-modern theory and practice has been debated among feminists in psychology, there has been less said about understanding women's *experience* of self/subjectivity (see Changing the Subject Collective, 1984; Hollway, 1989), and many would see notions of discourse and individual meaning and experience as inherently and irrefutably contradictory and thus incompatible.

This orthodoxy has been called to account within social psychology. Questions have been raised about the complex tension between a post-modern approach to gender–power relations, and the personal experience of subjectivity. My belief is that to exclude a *sense of the individual* from critical and feminist psychology is unproductive in the long term, and increases the widening gap between feminist psychologists and the women who might benefit from their analysis of gender–power relations (Dryden, 1998; Lewis, 1995b; Tunaley, 1995; Nicolson, 1994). However, I do not want to throw the baby out with the bath water! The theory and practice of discourse analysis has been exceptional in denting the positivist barriers of academic psychology, but is itself in danger of losing its grounding in everyday life (see Lewis, 1995a).

Practitioners and researchers alike need to accept that different kinds of research questions demand different approaches, and answers to the kinds of questions that qualitative research might address are in danger of being neglected. No amount of rigour in experimentation, sophisticated statistical techniques in survey methods or large-scale use of psychometric testing enables understanding of, for example, *what it feels like* to be depressed (Lewis, 1995a). The key point here is that practitioners and scientists need to know about both. At the present time knowledge of the 'what it feels like' type of question, essential for empathetic practice, is derived from anecdotal evidence and intuition. Qualitative methods have the capacity for both systematic and rigorous collection and analysis and as such potentially make a vital contribution to mental health knowledge.

Subjectivity, experience and meaning

How does an individual make sense of, monitor and account for her biography? What psychological processes is she able to draw upon to place experiences in context and give them meaning? Every woman has each of her children in the context of her own life and consequently each baby is conceived and born in a different context and for a different reason.

Frances would have been quite happy not to have any children, but Philip, her husband, had argued that

> a marriage was definitely in order to have children. Whereas for me it was good enough just to be married to Philip and children was not something so necessary ... and I wanted to marry Philip and to make sure it was *me* who married Philip.
>
> (Frances, Interview 1)

In contrast, Dion's partner did not want a baby. When he found out about the pregnancy, she said:

> he's not sort of over the moon. But he's not a person to show emotions.
>
> (Dion, Interview 1)

Samantha and her husband planned the pregnancy together, waiting first to move into a suitable house and finish decorating it. She then became pregnant quickly; others in the same situation, such as Lynn, had been trying to conceive for some time. However, for Lynn the pregnancy coincided with the axing of her post as a counsellor which prevented her getting depressed over that.

Shirley, who had not been keen on the idea of having a baby before, planned her pregnancy because her twin sister had had a baby the year before and so she considered it would be good to bring the cousins up together. There were as many reasons for conception and as many contexts as there were women in this study.

In the 1980s when this research began to take shape, there were almost no psychological precedents for explaining experience within such a framework. Sociologists had advanced the intellectual debates about gender, the family, childbirth and motherhood as I have outlined in the previous chapter and here above. However, psychological research was then (and to an extent still is) trapped within a framework of objectivity, while explanations of meaning were set within a crude psychoanalytic structure. Increasingly, I saw that traditional psychological approaches were inappropriate for my task.

Social psychology has now embraced a broadly post-modern, social constructionist perspective and its advocates are prepared to take a limited range of qualitative approaches to the discipline seriously. This privilege has been extended, particularly to discourse analysis and to some extent grounded theory. However, the relationship between experience and the agentic subject and the role of discourse remains contentious and the emphasis is upon social discourse rather than self and experience (see Doherty, 1994).

The emphasis in this book is firmly upon subjective knowledge, the meaning an individual places upon her own experience of childbirth and early motherhood in the context of her biography. This suggests that each pregnancy, delivery and baby potentially have a separate significance for each woman, although clearly each experience is informed by her own previous ones or those of close others. Similarly, negative feelings such as depression, feeling down, being fed up and so on need to be explained by each individual in terms of how they impinge upon her consciousness at the time of reporting them.

Subjective experience means more than just an idiosyncratic perception of events. It includes a conceptualisation of the whole person located in her biology, personal history and social world. Superimposed in this is a personal notion of 'reality' through which individuals interpret and make sense of their own lives. Thus the social world is filtered through a process of *reflexivity* through the double selectivity of (a) the individual's own location in the social structure and (b) their individual biography (Berger and Luckmann, 1985).

Making sense of meaning

'Meaning' is based upon what individuals count as knowledge, how they use that knowledge to make sense of experience and how that experience becomes incorporated into their biographies. Here I focus upon three aspects of this process – knowledgeability, reflexivity and the construction of biography, all of which are central to making sense of women's experiences of the transition to motherhood.

Giddens' knowledgeability and consciousness

Giddens (1984) offers a model which explains how individuals make sense of the social world in his theory of *structuration*. First he conceptualises human knowledgeability as occurring on three stratified levels. These are the levels of the practical consciousness, the discursive consciousness and the level of the unconscious.[5] Practical consciousness refers to those things which the individual *does*. It is essentially implicit knowledge. So, for example, to say 'I feel depressed' without applying close scrutiny to its meaning is practical consciousness. This does not imply that this simple statement indicates lack of thought or reflection. It is that it precedes it. Natasha felt that pregnancy was unpleasant because she saw herself as fat.

> I can't bear to look at myself in the mirror. Really I can't.
>
> (Natasha)

However, six months after the birth she emphasised:

> I probably thought I'd put on more weight than I actually did because I so hated being pregnant. I felt so fat and that Josh didn't really fancy me any more. I was frightened of that. But he was keen on me getting back to normal so he didn't say I looked nice fat.
>
> (Natasha)

In this extract Natasha is demonstrating a different level of consciousness, discursive consciousness, which is the intellectual level at which knowledge is experienced. At this level individuals *reflect* on what they know and do and also experience the contextual and ideological element in this knowledge.

Thus to say 'I feel depressed' might contain the key to someone's contextual understanding of depression. Some people might believe that to admit to depression because of certain feelings/experiences will gain them sympathy, or that it is a normal reaction to grief, having a baby, their own life circumstances and so on. Others may have comparable feelings but insist that they feel 'down', 'low' or 'fed up', or even deny such feelings because they do not believe that such an admission is becoming. Experience may modify one or both of these levels of consciousness. Thus, for Isobel talking about the fact that her baby had stopped her from putting her self first as she had done in the past:

> I don't resent the baby in any way. He was wanted but maybe I've always been a little bit selfish, and it takes time to adjust to that. I can't put me as number one.
>
> (Isobel)

This extract demonstrates a clear bridge between the practical and discursive levels of consciousness. She is presenting her thoughts both to herself and me, the interviewer, in order to make them acceptable (see Chapter 5).

---

5 These are directly related to Freud's ego, superego and id.

The unconscious level, which contains repressed cognitive and behavioural elements and by definition is unavailable to consciousness also impinges upon the other two levels. A person may 'give away' information that is inaccessible to them. Thus someone may say, 'I am not depressed,' but indicate a number of ways in which they may be observed to be depressed. In the extract above, Isobel, it seems, is also grappling with the intrusive unconscious. On that level she probably does resent the baby, but probably her resentment is directed more towards Graham, the baby's father.

> He's a fair-weather father. That's when the baby starts crying, it's time for mummy to do something about it! But that's got to change. I've got to retrain him. He was fantastic at first, then he probably started thinking I'm here all day, so it was probably my job to look after the baby. And if a nappy needs changing he'll say to me 'I think the nappy needs changing'. [*Laughs*]

The third time I interviewed Gwen (three months after the birth), she opened the door to let me in saying there was nothing to say because she was not depressed. However, she followed this by telling of a sequence of family funerals (including that of her own father, grandmother and a 13-year-old nephew of her husband's). She said that both she and her husband found the baby exciting and an important part of their life. I asked how her husband showed his interest in the baby and she said:

> It does not occur to him to say 'would you like a rest?'. I have to ask [*tension in her voice at this point*]. Having had a hard day at the office he'll come home and switch the box on and just sit. If he's holding Hazel – he'll just sit her on his lap – not really talk to her or anything. … I think it's easiest for us to learn – for the man it's tremendously difficult [see Chapter 5].

Giddens' theory of structuration also allows for a conceptualisation of time (*durée*) to indicate a continuous flow of conduct and cognition. He argues that purposive action is not composed of an aggregate or series of separate intentions, reasons and motives. Action is not a combination of acts; rather, acts are constituted only by a discursive moment of attention to the *durée* or lived-through experience. Action is rationalised through reflexivity, grounded in the continuous monitoring of action which human beings display and expect others to display.

Thus there is a sense in which action is understood temporarily as a continuous flow through 'biography'. This model therefore combines the concept of *durée* and levels of consciousness to locate action in a temporal, biographical and ideological context (see Chapter 5 for a fuller discussion of this).

Reflexivity

The reflexive process enables human beings to make sense of their actions and the context in which these actions occur – the immediate context and the context of the individual's life history. According to Mead (1934/67) reflexivity is 'the turning back of the experience of the individual upon himself [*sic*]' and thus the individual is able 'to take the attitude of the other toward himself … consciously to adjust himself to that process, and to modify the resultant of that process in any given social act in terms of his adjustment to it'. This is akin to 'having a conversation' with yourself. So, for example, the unnamed feeling someone might have, where they lack energy, see their life and the world pessimistically, is also experienced by that individual, in an attempt to make sense of the experience, *as if through the eyes of another*. This means the individual can in some way 'witness' their own actions/feelings and identify them (perhaps) as 'depression'. This series of conscious actions relies upon biography and past experience and also upon an understanding of 'knowledge' derived from social institutions and the cultural context. It is through reflexivity in this way that biography and self are created and recreated. 'Reflexiveness, then, is the essential condition, within the social process, for the development of mind' (Mead, 1934/67: 134).

The internal mechanisms that support Mead's thesis need further elucidation and are crucial to understanding how women explain their post-natal experiences to themselves and to the researcher – which I shall focus on in more detail in Chapter 5. Peter Ashworth (1979) suggested that there were two fundamental elements to the self in Mead's work: the *knower* and the *known*. This distinction, originally operationalised by William James (1892), had its origins in the philosophies of Schopenhauer and Kant, who recognised this dualistic structure of the conscious self. Mead equates these terms to the 'I' and the 'me'.

Mead (1934/67) drew a distinction between consciousness and self-consciousness in human experience which is useful for understanding internal 'conversation' and reflexivity. He was particularly interested in the way social interaction and the internalisation of how we see significant others evaluating our behaviour and beliefs influenced our self-conscious thoughts, and how those in turn were produced as a result of reflecting upon our consciousness. Thus:

> I talk to myself, and I remember what I said and perhaps the emotional content that went with it. The 'I' of this moment is present in the 'me' of the next moment. There again I cannot turn around quick enough to catch myself. I becomes a 'me' in so far as I remember what I said. The 'I' can be given, however, this functional relationship. It is because of the 'I' that we say that we are never fully aware of what we are, that we surprise ourselves by our own actions.
>
> (Mead, 1934/67: 174)

In other words, in order to be reflexive, we need to see our self as the 'object' of thought (i.e. 'me') but the seeing is done by 'I', the subject. The 'I' is impulsive and unorganised and equates to Freud's id, while the 'me', having come under social constraints, enables us to experience ourselves 'objectively' and account for our feelings and behaviour in a socially recognised way. Thus we can experience ourselves 'objectively' (the me/known) by the part of ourselves that is doing the experiencing 'subjectively' (the I/knower).

Pure experience is impulsive, but via a process of reflexivity the self as object becomes socialised. This is important when we are considering the meaning of the childbirth experience and depression, and probably accounts for some of the 'validity problems' of objective tests (Nicolson, 1986; Chapter 2). As there is no such thing as a unified, rational, homogeneous self, questions by those taking an objective stance are meaningless (see Chapter 5).

This cursory consideration of the composition of the self does not explain continuity of experience, which is important for understanding how the self/ identity develops and how actions and events (such as having a baby) take on a meaning within the context of self.

Symbolic interactionists, following Mead, saw self and society as interrelated, in that 'society' pre-dated 'mind', and 'mind' was the result of interaction between the individual and the social world. It is not relevant here to develop a critique of that view. All I want to do is draw attention to the indivisibility of the social and the self[6] to develop an explanation for why the event of childbirth cannot be seen apart from either the *individual experience* or the *cultural experience*.

Biography

The phenomenological sociologists of the 1960s were concerned to explain human experience in terms of individuals making their own sense of the world through the experience of constant interaction.

Experiences at each stage are given subjective meaning, and the meaning itself will have been interpreted and incorporated into the individual's accumulated biography, that is, 'The common sense view ... that we live through a certain sequence of events, some more and some less important, the sum of which is our biography' (Berger, 1966: 68). Thus the biography is experienced and understood within a prescribed social context, thus:

> The socially constructed world must be continually mediated to and actualised by the individual, so that it can become and remain indeed *his*[7] world as well. The individual is given by his society certain decisive

---

6 This goes beyond the scientists and clinicians offering social explanations of post-natal depression (Chapter 1). I am arguing for the constant interplay between the social and the self similar to the view expressed by Mead.

7 The term 'his' is in the original text. Original italics.

cornerstones for his everyday experience and conduct. Most importantly, the individual is supplied with specific sets of typifications and criteria for relevance, pre-defined for him by the society and made available to him for the ordering of his everyday life. This ordering … is biographically cumulative. It begins to be formed in the individual from the earliest stages of socialisation on, and then keeps on being enlarged and modified by himself throughout his biography.

(Berger and Kellner, 1964, in Anderson, 1982: 303)

The notion of biography therefore enables theorists and researchers to take account of current and retrospective considerations in the way people account for their lives, while individuals give meaning to their lives within a socially prescribed framework which takes account of social organisation and structure, including gender. Underlying the use of biography as a conceptual framework and methodological technique, is the view that the individual, others in her life, and the researcher may have different ideas about what is important and what is not, and these judgements are invariably made retrospectively.

Biography, then, provides a practical framework for understanding how accumulated experience may be interpreted and reinterpreted by the woman herself, thus giving an opportunity to understand the perspective of those who interact with her, or for whom she is a research subject or object of scrutiny.

Design

The design comprised a small-scale longitudinal study aimed to take account of change over the transition to motherhood and the post-natal period. Being longitudinal, the research enabled me to pay detailed attention to the dynamic process of becoming a mother, to allow me an opportunity to get to know the respondents and thus put the interviews into a context (see Chapter 5) and to make comparisons between women at various stages of the process.

It was necessarily small scale because of resource constraints – in terms of both the research time and budget and the anticipation that it would be difficult to recruit many women who could spare the time for several interviews.

There were important precedents at the time for intensive small-scale studies and subsequently there have been several more (e.g. Lewis, 1995b; Tunaley, 1995). As Rapoport and Rapoport (1976) had argued, 'results obtained from population studies or large-scale samples do *not* enable one to understand individual cases' (1976: 29).

I planned to interview twenty women on four occasions, because this would be both useful and manageable. In fact I recruited twenty-four women altogether (see respondent profiles in Appendix I).

The interviews were scheduled as indicated in Table 1.

The timing of the post-natal interviews was arbitrary to an extent, although the timing was expected to distinguish between the immediate post-natal period, a potentially stable time at three months, when physical and emotional recovery

Table 1 Timing and content of interviews

Interview 1
Soon after recruitment – during pregnancy
Retrospective account of social and biographical context

Interview 2
One month after the birth
Account of labour, birth and the early post-natal period

Interview 3
Three months after the birth
Account of the period from interview 2 onwards, but to include a
retrospective account of month one

Interview 4
Six months after the birth
Account of the period from interview 3 onwards, but to include a
retrospective account of months over the transition to motherhood

---

from labour should have occurred, and at six months when it would be reasonable to expect a resolution of any earlier emotional lability. Because of the constraints explained above, the first interview, which was to be during pregnancy, was to take place at whatever stage I could recruit a participant.

Conclusion

The experience of conducting these interviews in the context of being 'steeped' in the literature on PND facilitated an important learning process. It enabled me to understand that research is primarily about raising and answering questions you set yourself or which emerge from the existing science. There is no value-free knowledge. Mainstream research on PND had a mission and so did I. The investment that medical scientists have in ensuring that PND is seen as both distinct from other depressions and as a psychiatric disorder is being challenged by evidence from practitioners who have talked to women. Practitioner-based research indicates that there is not necessarily a unified, rational entity PND. However, it continues to be defined as an 'illness', even though epidemiologically the incidence[8] of psychotic problems remains relatively rare.

4

POST-NATAL CARE AND 'MATERNITY BLUES'

... human childbirth is accomplished in and shaped by culture, both in a general sense and in the particular sense of the varying definitions of reproduction offered by different cultures. How a society defines reproduction is closely linked with its articulation of women's position: the connections between female citizenship and the procreative role are social not biological.

(Oakley, 1980: 6)

Introduction

The rhetoric surrounding childbirth and motherhood reflects the belief that the birth of a baby is a 'happy event' and that motherhood itself is a universally fulfilling experience for women. The ideological implications of these beliefs have been well documented by feminist writers (Oakley, 1980; Phoenix *et al.*, 1991) and are discussed in Chapter 1.

In western societies childbirth usually takes place in hospital, which means that women's experience of pregnancy and the first hours and days of motherhood are circumscribed within a medically managed framework (Niven, 1992). Consequently, an unease evolves between the competing requirements of mothers and attending clinicians, in that, for the majority of women, pregnancy and birth are about having a baby and becoming a mother; for the doctors, successful action is the delivery of a healthy baby and (as far as possible) mother (Graham and Oakley, 1981).

Furthermore, additional tension frequently exists between midwives and obstetricians, who favour contrasting models of delivery: the former, independent practitioners fully qualified to take charge of the maternity care of a woman undergoing a 'normal' delivery; the latter, often having less experience of normal childbirth, but being qualified to intervene if the pregnancy or labour appear not to be proceeding to plan.

This chapter explores the tension between the way that birth is managed and described, particularly in relation to the concept of 'maternity blues', experiences of labour, childbirth and the immediate post-natal period. It arises out of the theoretical implications derived from the discussions in the preceding chapters, through considering the psychological experience of becoming a mother, in the context of biography, gender relations, culture and subjective experience.

Birth, hormones and the blues?

Harriette Marshall outlined the ways in which 'expert' manuals seek to provide women with a normal pattern of reactions to the transition to motherhood, from birth through the early months and years of mothering (Marshall, 1991). Following childbirth, women are expected to become 'emotional' and experience 'maternity blues' or the 'baby blues', characterised by temporary mood swings including depression and weeping (see Oakley, 1980; Chapter 2 in this volume). According to experts: 'the "blues", experienced by a majority of women, are either inexplicable, irrational, "women's troubles" or they are explained in terms of women being at the mercy of their hormones, experiencing hormonal "imbalance" or "chaos"' (Marshall, 1991: 71). This type of information is so commonplace and widespread that it was familiar to all the respondents in this study. The focus of the second interview (around one month after delivery) was upon perceptions of the birth and the period immediately after it[1] and at that time, twenty-two of a total of twenty-three (i.e. 95%) reported some experience of depression, anxiety or weeping. This is consistent with findings from clinical studies (e.g. Pitt, 1968). Does this mean they were all victims of their raging hormones? Each respondent who described episodes of weeping, spontaneously rejected the idea that it was because they had the 'blues' or 'depression'. The clearly recognisable, everyday discourse surrounding the 'baby blues' was both acknowledged and legitimised by the participants, while at the same time they distanced themselves from it. Instead, each gave detailed explanations of what led to their behaviours. They contextualised them within the varied events over the days and weeks following childbirth, making their own reactions logical and meaningful, but outside the 'blues' discourse. Their explanations are shown in Table 2 below.

This table suggests a picture at odds with the predominant medical view that post-natal mood swings are associated exclusively with hormone fluctuations. While my study did not set out to discredit biochemical explanations,[2] it does propose that mood swings *do not occur in a vacuum* and therefore to conceptualise them as a direct consequence of hormonal imbalance must be seen to be (at least) problematic. Having a baby and being in hospital are both socially and psychologically stressful experiences during which the woman having the baby experiences pain and uncertainty. Any emotional responses need to be considered as rational, whether or not hormones make the individual more vulnerable to depression. As Christine Jelabi puts it: 'Very few women, particularly if their experience of childbirth has been painful, prolonged or complicated, will feel at their best post-natally' (Jelabi, 1993: 59).

It is clear that birth is painful and stressful, whatever the outcome. Women

---

1 In certain cases details of the birth were discussed again at a later stage. This was particularly true, for example, with women such as Hilary and Jerri, both of whom had been especially upset by the experience.

2 The design is not appropriate and I did not set out to test this hypothesis.

Table 2 Interview 2: explanations of depression/weeping during the first post-natal month

(a) Midwives' behaviour on labour ward $n = 7$ 30.4%	(b) Pain & exhaustion $n = 22$ 95%
(c) Hospital staff's treatment of baby $n = 7$ 30.4%	(d) Anxiety about baby care/breast-feeding $n = 9$ 39.7%
(e) Midwives' behaviour/rudeness/ lack of sympathy on post-natal ward $n = 17$ 74%	(f) Negative responses to the 'bonding' discourse $n = 17$ 74%
(g) Adjustment to homecoming/ incompetence $n = 12$ 52.1%	(h) No rational reason $n = 0$ 0%

usually go into labour when they have had around nine months of excitement, worry, uncertainty about the baby, are exhausted from carrying increased weight and generally, especially towards the end, desperate for the experience to be over and done. More than anything labour can be a frightening experience because of the uncertainty at each stage, and women ask themselves: how long will it last, how painful will it be, how well will I handle the pain, will the staff be competent and what will I think of the baby?

Few find labour easy, although most had optimistic expectations about how they would manage the process.

> I tried to do the breathing as much as I could stand it and then I couldn't stand it and had the gas and air.
>
> (Samantha)

> In the end, quite honestly, I couldn't have cared if they had cut off my head I was so tired.
>
> (Penelope)

> One thing that surprised me [about the labour] was the amount of screaming and shouting I did. I thought I'd be very controlled – like a film I saw. I was surprised, but I found it helped.
>
> (Lynn)

> Oh my God. I can't imagine anything harder. ... Once all the pain ceased and I just lay there feeling tired – that was a tremendous relief.
>
> (Gwen)

> I thought 'this is it!'. I was really scared.
>
> (Matilda, on describing her emergency Caesarean)

All the women in the study had taken the business of labour very seriously and tried their best to meet standards they had set themselves, which corresponded with the philosophy of the time – that as far as possible pain relief should be 'natural' and that labour should be allowed to progress as normally as possible for as long as possible. However, as can be seen from the table in Appendix I, not all succeeded.

In what follows I draw out the contrast between women's accounts of their immediate post-natal experience and the notion of irrational responses to hormone changes. What is routinely taken to be the period of 'the maternity blues' is characterised here by accounts of extreme resilience under pressure. No one exhibited weepiness 'for no reason' and many reported good reasons why they might be extremely distressed. The following extracts illustrate the respondents' explanations.[3]

Anxiety about the midwives' behaviour during labour

Labour is an exhausting, painful and potentially frightening experience. In an early study of maternity staff I found that midwives and mothers had conflicting interests. Midwives believed that the delivery of a healthy baby was their prime objective, which often made them impatient with women screaming and making a fuss (see Nicolson, 1983). This attitude of some midwives impinged in an extreme way upon some women's experiences of labour.

> All these things started to go wrong, and about midnight (I'd had an epidural as I couldn't take any more pain) I was told I was going to have a Caesarean. I actually thought, 'I'm going to die now'. ... Tom [the baby's father and live-in partner] said he wanted to come with me, but the horrible nurses said, 'Are you married?' ... 'You can't come in then!' He insisted. I was terrified. I was absolutely petrified.
>
> (Jerri, Interview 2)

This experience haunted and disturbed Jerri who retold it to me at the subsequent interviews, when she also reiterated her anger and told me of recurrent dreams about the birth and the way she and Tom were treated.

Some midwives' behaviour could be described as 'brutal':

> Labour was marred by a particularly unpleasant midwife. She didn't introduce herself. ... I had been promised that the notes on my bad back

---

3 To quantify the data I read the text of the transcripts and developed a set of categories for each of the different explanations for the depression, weeping and anxiety they described. I then did a simple counting exercise for explanations within each categ ry. Several women gave more than one explanation.

injury would be given to the person on duty. But she ignored my pleas to sit up, and I had a brutal internal.

(Sylvia, Interview 2)

The consequences for both these women were that they felt they had been 'invalidated' by these experiences, which made them feel anxious and helpless, reinforcing the power relationship between the midwives and themselves.

Reactions to pain and tiredness

... once the initial relief of a safe delivery has worn off, exhaustion and discomfort are apt to take over. When these feelings are combined with the round-the-clock caring of a new baby, it is perhaps inevitable that a mother would appear to be depressed.

(Jelabi, 1993: 59)

For many women the pain of labour is a shock despite preparation classes. Lynn, Norma and Gwen, all of whom had planned home deliveries, had been admitted to hospital during labour because of the pain and duration of labour. Lynn had been surprised by the 'amount of screaming and shouting I did' and the pain and worry had made her feel 'past caring'. Gwen had thought, 'Oh my God – I can't imagine anything harder.' Norma (an experienced midwife) had felt violent towards anyone who approached her. She felt that the pain was 'frightful'.

While it is considered normal for a surgical patient to be depressed and anxious after an operation (see Revans, 1968, for a classic study of this), women's emotionality following labour is still attributed to hormones rather than a response to the pain, shock, anaesthetic and pain-numbing drugs.

However, the women themselves considered that lack of sleep and pain rendered their reactions justifiable.

The only time I was ever tearful in hospital was when we'd had a bad night, and at 4 a.m. when I'd been on the go for three hours, I finally rang the buzzer and asked the nurse to take him away because I was exhausted. Once I'd done that it was a great relief.

(Sharon, Interview 2)

Jerri had felt that her body had been so violated that she never wanted anyone to touch it again.

That included changing my sanitary towels. I could not bear anyone near me. ... I'd been through so much and I was in pain.

(Jerri, Interview 2)

Hilary, following a difficult birth and a larger than average episiotomy, said:

I was badly swollen and bruised and could only lie on one side. Two stitches opened. I was really cross. I was so bruised. I couldn't pass urine. I just felt upset and miserable. I had a tube put in. On the third day they took it out. I went to the loo. I managed to be able to lie on my tummy. But I couldn't sleep for pain. The following morning they examined me. The damned stitches had opened up. I was miserable then. I really cried.

(interview 2)

This kind of physical mutilation under any other circumstances would be considered a reasonable cause of anxiety and depression. However, the physical trauma of birth is habitually ignored when causes of maternity 'blues' are being considered. Although pain and tiredness are acknowledged by experts as part of the childbirth process, their relevance to depression, until very recently, is not. In this study the women identify pain, sleep deprivation and mood swings as interconnected and as rational explanations for outward behaviours such as weeping and inward ones such as anxiety and depression.

Hospital staff's treatment of the baby

Several midwives in hospital did not live up to the mothers' expectations in their care of the baby, which was a source of great concern. There was a common belief that midwives were experts on baby care and so it came as a shock to some women when they considered that their babies were not being well treated. In the case of Lynn's baby, who had been placed under observation after swallowing his own waste matter during delivery, she became shocked and disillusioned when

We went to visit him in the nursery. We thought it would be a place with a few babies and staff, but their so-called nursery was basically a store room ... he was there on his own and a nurse popped in every four hours. ... We were in a dreadful state.

(Lynn, Interview 2)

Other mothers were worried about the level and extent of explanations they received about infant crying, feeding and other behaviours and felt that they were sometimes made to worry (perhaps unecessarily) in the face of what they perceived as the staff's lack of vigilance and care towards the baby.

Anxiety about baby-care, particularly breast-feeding

New mothers, steeped in the rhetoric discussed in Chapter 1, expected breast-feeding to be natural and simple – in accord with the peaceful and satisfying Madonna and infant of classic and popular mythology.

> The current trend towards breast feeding is due, in part, to the emer-
> gence of various middle-class campaigning groups ... which have stressed
> the benefits of breast feeding for both mother and child. Health visitors
> and doctors often advise women that by breast feeding their infants they
> will not only provide them with proper nutrition and certain immunities,
> but will also encourage the process of 'bonding' to take place.
>
> (Richardson, 1993: 10–11)

Thus a great deal is at stake. Breast-feeding in particular, then, was an issue over
which success or failure brought about extreme feelings for some women.

Frances had problems with her nipples, which meant she had to both express
milk and use plastic teats on her nipples at various times. This caused her
emotional distress, which was exacerbated when eventually she had to give these
procedures up and bottle-feed.

Penelope found herself a victim of expert advice.

> Breast-feeding became a nightmare. I was bombarded by different in-
> structions and advice ... then she seemed to be thriving on my milk and
> milk from the milk bank. Then they suddenly said, 'Oh we haven't got
> any more', with virtually no warning. I found that devastating. That was
> really awful. Everyone said breast milk was best, and then to have the
> supply cut off was a bit much – I got very upset over that.
>
> (Penelope, Interview 2)

Not everyone felt so strongly, however. Both Melanie and Jane found that bottle-
feeding enabled longer intervals between feeds, and for Melanie in particular the
choice of bottle-feeding meant that she and her partner could share the tasks
equally, resulting in her being less exhausted than was the case with some of the
other participants (see below in this chapter and later in Chapter 5 for a further
discussion of the 'bonding' discourse).

Staff behaviour on the post-natal wards

Several women were distressed because of staff behaviour on the post-natal ward.
This included contradictory advice, rudeness and lack of sympathy.

While Jane had been in hospital, she had received thoughtless treatment in
relation to breast-feeding problems, nappy changing and bathing the baby. After
delivery she had tried to introduce the baby to the breast, but it had been difficult
and the staff just left her, despite her requests for help.

> I probably wasn't doing it properly and I was very disappointed.
>
> (Jane, Interview 2)

Later in the ward she tried again but got no support from the midwives, only from

60

some of the other mothers. Jane was in hospital for five days and quickly developed high blood pressure, which she attributed to the stress of being in hospital, so much so that she had a row with the doctor who told her she had to remain there until the problem was sorted out.

> I was weak. I really felt terrible. It got to the point on Monday – they said, 'Wait until tomorrow.' I couldn't stand it and said, 'Look if you don't let me go home I'm going to discharge myself.' The baby was fine. I knew that it was because I hadn't slept. Anxiety. They offered me my own room. I said it wouldn't make any difference. 'OK then,' they said. 'If anything happens it's not down to us.' I said, 'That's my risk.' But I knew. The next morning, or the morning after, I was checked and the night I came home she slept through the night and I felt wonderful. I really did. And they checked my blood pressure and it was right back to normal.
>
> (Jane, Interview 2)

Midwives' responses after the baby was born varied. On the whole, the women in this study did not find the hospital midwives very helpful, although the small number of women who had arranged to be under the care of a named or independent midwife were very positive (see Table AI).

However, Sarah found good support from the hospital midwives too:

> They were excellent all the midwives. Without exception. They were so good and sensitive. On the first day I got into a real state changing his nappy and just burst into tears. No one saw me doing that but after I asked to speak to someone and started crying again she pulled the curtains round and wasn't at all patronising – giving me advice and sympathy.
>
> (Sarah)

This is exactly what women wanted – recognition that they were capable of the tasks of looking after a new baby, alongside the acknowledgement that they did not have innate capacities:

> Everyone was looking over my shoulder to see how I was handling the baby, and in some ways I was much more comfortable once I had got home – but then I've got to learn and I've never had a baby before.
>
> (Isobel)

> They left her with me. That was awful 'cos I didn't expect that. They just left the cot and I thought, 'God what do I do?' I didn't know whether they'd wake me to feed her so I couldn't sleep worrying about her and I did think it's a bit of an anti-climax anyway because you feel a bit drained and you think, 'Oh is this it? What do I do with her?' No one explained

anything at that stage. It was during the night. It was awful, but she started crying and I was worried about handling her. I felt groggy as well because of the drugs so I rang the bell and the nurse picked her up and was a bit short and said, 'Oh she doesn't need feeding yet.' She just held her and talked to her and then she went to sleep again.

(Samantha)

Negative responses to the 'bonding' discourse

Because motherhood is seen almost entirely as instinctual, it is considered natural for mothers to love and 'bond' with their infants and such emotions are viewed as the central core of motherhood.

(Woollett, 1991: 41)

Many respondents were worried that they felt nothing for the baby when it was born and therefore that they would have difficulty with 'bonding'. Maternity hospitals espouse the dominant view that human mothers need to be actively enabled to form an early attachment with their infant, which is achieved through close physical contact immediately on delivery and through subsequent close proximity. This is based upon the view that such attachment is instinctual, but might be disrupted if the infant is removed too soon after birth to the nursery (Klaus and Kennell, 1976; see Chapter 1). Popular awareness of this 'bonding' discourse and the expectation of the sudden emergence of natural love towards the newborn infant has led to a 'self-pathologisation' in the harsh light of personal experience.

It was a really strange feeling, and I expected to feel something for her and I didn't. I kept thinking, 'Oh God – a total stranger!' I didn't feel anything.

(Samantha, Interview 2)

And later:

... they left her with me. That was awful. ... I thought this was the worst thing I'd ever done – had a baby and felt nothing.

(Samantha, Interview 2)

Felicity, whose baby was three weeks early, said:

I was pretty stunned. ... I'd been getting ready for Christmas, and all of a sudden I was sitting on a table with this stranger between my knees! ... I didn't have any instant maternal thing at all.

(Felicity, Interview 2)

Also:

My body felt wrecked. I felt so much pain and was so exhausted that this little baby didn't mean much to me.

(Norma, Interview 2)

Jerri said that she swore at her son when she first saw him, and Meg, who had nearly died from a haemorrhage during the birth, did not feel anything for her baby.

I just went numb. … I remember the midwife said 'Oh it's a boy. Did you want a boy?' The question was just meaningless to me.

(Meg, Interview 2)

However, these were their retrospective stories: by the time I interviewed them when the baby was around one month old, they all reported that they were deeply attached to their infants.

Adjustments to bringing the baby home and feelings of incompetence

Returning home from hospital, although frequently perceived as a longed-for relief, was often a shock to the respondents. Isobel found that coming home made her feel as if she were 'in a daze – completely in a daze … it was a bit of a shock' (Interview 2).

Frances also reported that 'it was all a shock', even though she had had a baby previously. She had, however, made a prior decision to stay in hospital as long as possible in order to rest, based on her experience on the last occasion.

An extreme case was Wendy, whose husband could not bear to hear the baby cry. He took two weeks' paternity leave but did renovation work on the house rather than look after either Wendy or the baby. She therefore found herself doing all the cooking and cleaning as well as infant care. She was thus also 'in a daze, a complete daze' and 'it was a bit of a shock' (Interview 2).

Reasons for sad feelings after birth and shortly after arriving home were also connected with the new, strange experience of feeling responsible but incompetent. Frances felt incompetent and anxious with the responsibilities incumbent upon her with a baby and an older child.

I'm not good at mothering, nurturing, whatever. I'm hopeless at giving baths. … My brain is like a colander. I can only hold one thought in it at a time.

(Frances, Interview 2)

Sharon similarly declared:

My brain is so befuddled. I can't remember long words.

(Sharon, Interview 2)

The need to 'manage' others or the problems they caused was high on the agenda as a cause of distress. Those needing managing included other family members, friends, the nanny or maternity nurse.

> [The maternity nurse] turned out to be a disaster ... she was quiet, rather superior, always tended to look down her nose at you. I felt embarrassed.
>
> (Sylvia, Interview 2)

Gwen talked about a (grand)mother who was supposed to be giving support:

> Mother made endless cups of tea and didn't do anything to help. I kept thinking, 'Be nice to your mother!' but I was getting more and more agitated. We desperately needed someone to do the shopping, and I was irritated by the way she waited around at mealtimes.
>
> (Gwen, Interview 2)

Gwen had to send her mother away eventually.

Lynn claimed that if she had not had six weeks of continuous support she would not have coped without experiencing depression. She had felt extremely tired and anxious, particularly after the early worries about the birth and the baby. Her parents, both of whom were close friends, her grandmother and her husband were with her in various combinations all the time. She said that she had hardly changed a nappy for all that time. Her parents did all the washing, shopping and cooking and her mother always went with her to clinic appointments. At one point when it seemed she might have to be alone for two days she decided she did not want to manage and her grandmother came to fill in the gap. It was

> just the sheer tiredness. It was just feed, nappy, feed, nappy. I've been absolutely exhausted. My grandmother came down early because I couldn't face two days on my own.

The support meant that:

> He's changed my life – yes – but he hasn't absolutely taken it over. He gets a lot of attention – but I still have a life of my own.

For different reasons, because they were sharing the infant care equally, Melanie and her husband John resisted help from relatives and friends because they knew they could help each other better than anyone else could help them. The degree and quality of support in the early months of mothering was probably the most crucial factor in a woman's emotional survival.

Control over birth: reflecting on the experience

The subjective evaluation of the quality of the birth experience is difficult to measure. It was, however, a key issue for everyone interviewed. A serious question for several women was about control in labour – either not being in control because the whole process was different from that anticipated or because of an unforeseen medical problem. Lack of control made them disappointed and sometimes ashamed, particularly if they felt they had let themselves down by their behaviour.

Melanie, who had found the midwives very supportive, said:

> They let me push for three hours and I was in quite a state. Gas and air did nothing! Either I wasn't breathing right or I didn't get it at the right time in a contraction. I felt it was painful but I could have coped better. But it was unlike any pain I've had before.
>
> (Melanie, Interview 2)

The baby's head became stuck and the midwives had tried to avoid an episiotemy because they would have to twist her hip as she was severely arthritic. They eventually did do one and the baby was born soon afterwards. Melanie felt she had handled labour badly and ought to have been more in control.

> It's hard to be rational. I've forgotten or not registered a lot but I could have been better in control. … You must take leave of your senses. I had no concept of time.
>
> (Melanie, Interview 2)

Shirley, who had planned an induced hi-tech labour, felt totally in control, which conflicts with empirical evidence (see Cartwright, 1979). Shirley, as arranged, started labour at 9.00 a.m. and her baby was born early evening.

> I had nothing against induction. The whole process was friendly and relaxed – nothing happened when the membrane was burst, so they put me on a drip. The consultant couldn't find the vein, which amused everybody and then the new machine didn't work so they had to bring in the old one.
>
> (Shirley, Interview 2)

The pain, however, became unbearable.

> I started on nothing and fairly quickly decided to go for an epidural, so I was moved from the room I was in. The anaesthetist was rather incompetent and had to try six or seven times to get the needle into the spine. The worst thing was they had to slow things down, but it didn't work and then they tried pethidine. It did upset me.
>
> (Shirley, Interview 2)

This style of delivery, in this case, had given Shirley a sense of personal control despite the pain. She was pleased because she gave birth within the 'working day' and on a prearranged date.

Hilary, who had had a Caesarean for the birth of her first child, was determined to be more in control this time. The Caesarean had meant a sense of loss. During this delivery the pain became very bad, very quickly.

> I just felt out of control really. The pains were quite bad and they had to slow me down at one stage I was contracting so fast. I thought I was dying. I kept telling Ken, 'This is impossible.' I don't think I was talked to enough. They were there, but not engaging me in conversation and Ken was just upset to think that I was in pain. ... So that was the birth. I was much more out of control than I imagined. You have these ideas you will say more, do more, contribute more, but I was in too much pain most of the time to do anything. I mean I had coped.
>
> (Hilary, Interview 2)

Similarly, Angela had suffered months of distress after feeling that she had handled the birth of her first son badly. She had screamed and cried and felt out of control, which had left her with a prolonged sense of shame and guilt. She found her second experience far more satisfying and her sense of control meant for her that the immediate post-natal experience was far more positive, including the initial attitude to her baby.

Conclusion

Having a baby and becoming a mother are not the same kind of experience for women. Each baby a woman has is a different experience on each occasion. This is not only because of the circumstances surrounding birth but because each baby occurs at a different stage of a woman's biography. In addition, having a baby is not the only thing that happens to her at that time – life goes on around her regardless. Childbirth is not an independent variable around which other variables may be controlled for. The transition to motherhood is deeply embedded in a woman's life experience and her particular circumstances.

However, having a baby is very much a gendered experience and it is something that women have in common even if they never become mothers. Motherhood is a status through which women's lives are defined. Thus, whether a woman becomes a mother or not, she and others see her as a potential mother or someone who has failed (for whatever reason) to become a mother. Whether a woman remains a mother full-time or succeeds in a career, she has to concern herself in some way with the role of mother. For these reasons motherhood is a central part of the female identity. Women have to experience themselves *as* a woman in the sense prescribed through the dominant culture. Thus they constantly evaluate themselves against their ability to mother and others' assessment of that ability.

The transition to motherhood is an intersection between the psychological, the social, the biological and the temporal. It is essential that it is understood in this way by scientists and clinical practitioners if they are to make sense of the concept of PND from a woman's perspective.

5

REFLEXIVITY, INTERVENTION
AND THE CONSTRUCTION OF
POST-NATAL DEPRESSION

Introduction

This chapter explores the research *process*, through examining the impact of the interview itself on the respondent, mediated by the interviewer. The *interaction* between the respondent and interviewer at various stages throughout the process is the *mechanism* through which PND is constructed via a meaning shared and understood by both. This is defined through the way that both participants (i.e. researcher and respondent) enable the respondent to *reflect* upon that activity and engagement.

As the basis for this chapter I employ some detailed interview extracts, first to illuminate key issues on how post-natal depression is constructed through the way the women account for *themselves* and second to assess the way the interviewer made connections between their *everyday lives* and the *professional discourses* surrounding childbirth, motherhood and post-natal depression.

Doing qualitative research

Bott's (1957) study of families and social networks was an important source of inspiration for the rationale and design of this study. Her work was significant in the history of applied psychological research because first she demonstrated an awareness of the *effects of social interaction* between families and between families and interviewers over time. Second, she was aware of research itself as a *dynamic social process* whereby changes in the researcher's conceptual orientation develop as the research itself progresses. Third, she problematised concepts traditionally taken for granted, such as the 'normal' family, 'culture', 'class'. Finally, she attempted to integrate sociological and psychological ideas as well as employ psychoanalytic ideas.[1]

It was almost thirty years later that Markova (1985) reiterated the need to focus on the social and dynamic qualities of social research. She argued that social

---

1 She was, however, relatively unquestioning about women's familial status. See Nicolson (1988: 80–4) for a discussion of Bott's work.

psychology should take account of a research design that 'incorporates the inter-action between A and B and not just the influence of B on A. Secondly, that the research is designed in such a way that data are primarily of a qualitative i.e. conceptual rather than quantitative nature' (1985: 6). The reason for conducting my research in this way has been discussed in detail elsewhere (Nicolson, 1986; 1988; Chapter 3). I considered, both at the time I designed this study and now, that traditional psychological research almost never achieves its own ends – that is to be objective, value free and not impact on the personalities of the 'experi-menter' or their 'subjects' upon the 'experimental' or research relationship. Fur-ther, I came to believe in the course of doing this study that the complexities of people's lives are more than simply a set of variables, however extensively these variables may be identified and controlled for.

These complexities are present not only in the *accounts* elicited as data but in the *interactions* which take place as data are collected. Each encounter between the experimenter and subject, researcher and respondent, whoever they are and for however limited the research period, exists in a number of dimensions – all of which may be explained through the sociological framework discussed in Chapter 3. Mead's work on the self as 'subject' and 'object' promotes understanding of how an interview is not simply a means of collecting qualitative data on tape and later analysis as a transcribed text. Talking to another human being brings indi-vidual and shared consciousness into play, and thus reflexive, discursive and un-conscious dimensions to the encounter (Chapter 3).

In the example that follows, Norma – through talking to me – shows her am-bivalence about herself becoming a mother. She focuses away from the potential pleasures and growth that a baby might mean and considers whether or not a baby is the end of 'self' or whether it is possible to live through the baby to get to the other side. She divides 'mother' from 'person'. She has a view of what a 'good mother' is and does. The good *mother* gives herself up to the baby, while a good *person*, as exemplified by herself as she is now and her non-mother friends, is independent and free. That independence is so separate from the 'mother' that she believes that becoming a mother will bring about her rejection.

NORMA: I kind of thought that if I have a baby, that's the end of me as a person. I'd never be able to do anything again and I suppose one of my sisters is a single mother and she's gone on to university. And she was very supportive ... and said there's life afterwards! I think that helped a lot.

PAULA: What made you think that way?

NORMA: Well, I don't know. I don't have many friends who have babies. The women I work with have babies. I just look after women and babies for seven days and then they go back into the community.[2] But you see women on buses with pushchairs – and I think of my own experience of my own mother. She

2 Norma is a midwife.

was a midwife and gave up work to have children and her whole life revolved around us. I felt that – it's a very Irish thing I suppose – but to be a good mother I'd have to be at home all the time to really give myself. And I just liked to have my freedom, and as I say most of my friends are very independent. And I thought … well they won't want to know me. My friends won't want to be around me and a crying baby. You go to a party and there's a woman with a baby. In a way she is excluded. She ends up running after the baby – feeding, changing it. It's different you know. I was very frightened. I thought this is it. I'm just going to come to a stop and I didn't think I'd be able to organise myself enough to do all the things I wanted to do.

(Interview 1, page 3)

Gwen, in the next example, demonstrates contradiction and unconscious conflict in her account of her husband's role as father.

PAULA: Is she equally central to both of you?

GWEN: Yes, definitely.

PAULA: That must be a support to you. How does his interest manifest itself?

GWEN: When he comes home in the evening he'll want to take over and give me a rest. If I want to go out he's more than happy to look after her, change nappies and all the rest of it. And she does take bottles, so if I want a rest I'll go and make a bottle and he'll do it.

I was just exhausted yesterday. I felt totally drained by the time I got up in the morning and I wanted to go back to bed. But there were things to do and people to see so I couldn't really.

PAULA: So going back to your husband. There's no complaint on your side that he's leaving you to cope alone?

GWEN: Well sometimes … general little niggles. Um, if he comes in and I suppose he's got so used to me breast feeding that it doesn't occur to him to say, 'would you like a rest?' I have to *ask* and having had a hard day at the office, he'll come home and switch the box on and just sit. And if he's holding her he'll just sit her on his lap. Not really talk to her or anything. And if I'm downstairs I can hear her whingeing and crying. It sets me on edge. I'll storm back upstairs and say, 'She's a little human being you know, she does get bored. Talk to her!' But apart from that he is beginning to learn that he has to show her things around the room to hold her attention or else she'll start crying again. I think it's easier for us to learn. For the men it's tremendously difficult. … I'm here all day. He doesn't think about it.

This extract, which is overtly on Giddens' *practical* level of consciousness, intended to demonstrate her husband's mutual concern about the baby, is heavily underpinned by anger towards him for neglect of the baby and thus herself (see Chapter 7). As she reflects and develops her account, her use of language betrays to me and to herself that she is exhausted. What began as a discussion of a 'good father' slips into a description of a man who 'helps out'. Even when he does take over and feed the baby, Gwen has to make up the bottle. She deals with this eventually at the end of this extract by talking of gender differences in ability in relation to child-care.

As Giddens' work emphasised, conversations operate on more than one level and develop and flow over time. That *time* occurs not only during the interviews but in anticipation and on reflecting on them by both participants and at various stages. For the respondent, to be asked about themselves and their self in relation to the transition to motherhood demands discursive and reflexive engagement. This in turn occurs in a context where a relationship between interviewer and respondent is developing, with all that means about perceiving self and others. Further, the interviewer–respondent interaction is constructing, via the interview, a new set of relationships and social statuses for the respondent (see Chapter 6).

For the interviewer, there are the multiple anxieties about whether and how the encounter will work – will rapport be established, will the respondent have anything to say and will the questions be well constructed and received? Thinking about the interview retrospectively brings both the respondent and interviewer more opportunity for reflexivity, although their aims are different. The interviewer will have the tape and transcript to focus on as well as the memory of certain aspects of the encounter and the 'atmosphere'. The respondent will have been stimulated to contextualise her life in relation to the experience of having this baby and this process will probably be carried over into the subsequent interviews. Finally, the data are a product of the *subjectivity of both participants* in the *context of their social worlds* populated by significant others and also *products of their biographies*.

Reflexivity in action

One central aspect of the interview in qualitative research is *reflexivity* (see Chapter 3). This has been defined by researchers in a number of ways (Doherty, 1994) and for those engaged in symbolic interactionist, feminist, post-modern or social constructionist projects this continues to be a highly contentious but key concept (see Banister *et al.*, 1994).

Reflexivity in the research interview accounts for and respects 'the different meanings brought to the research by researcher and volunteer' (Parker in Banister *et al.*, 1995: 14). This assumes the potential for the shared understanding of events or emotional experience, and that the participants experience a sense of meaning *prior* to the research encounter.

Alternatively, it may be used to confirm a relativist position, i.e. that *talk* between respondent and interviewer is functional in *creating* what might be seen as individual, prior experiences and meanings, that 'taking reflexivity seriously in doing research is marked by a concern for recognising that constructing is a social process, rooted in language, not located inside one's head' (Steier, 1991: 5).

Here, however, it is used in a way that assumes an individual with a biography and a dynamic sense of her/his life's meaning (Nicolson, 1988; 1994).[3] In the following extract from an interview with Felicity this process can be seen in detail.

PAULA: What made you decide to have a baby at this stage?
FELICITY: It's been a long process. A rather boring story.
PAULA: Not to me!
FELICITY: When we got married, Martin had had one by a previous marriage. He didn't want to have any more children and I acknowledged this, and assumed we had come to some agreement. I didn't worry about it, but actually once we'd got married he decided he wanted children but I didn't know this. We understood one another on one level but not on another. Then we carried on quite a long dialogue – not really understanding each other. When I tried to think about it, it got harder and harder to make a decision. What happened I think is that I tried to take it all on myself, and I tried actually to work it out so that I could carry on working and in the end I just gave up. I couldn't think any more. I had put so much energy into thinking about it that I gave up.

(Interview 1)

Felicity, through being asked to tell me about her decision to have a baby, actively engaged in evaluating her thoughts and behaviours. She focused on the thoughts she had as she believed she had done, at the time she first had them and now, retrospectively. Evidence that this is what is going on in the interactive–reflexive process may be derived from the observation that I might find her ideas boring, through to her reflections on her relationship with Martin and his views on parenthood.

My own reasons for doing this research were also personal and the topic was and continues to be of great interest to me, although the underlying reason for my interest has shifted – from recollections of my own experiences and trying to make sense of them to trying to make sense of the respondents' lives. Now my preoccupation lies more in attempting to influence the academic and clinical communities into paying attention to what women are saying about the transition to motherhood. A precedent for this was set by Judi Marshall:

I have always chosen as research topics issues which have personal significance and which I need to explore in my own life. ... This involvement provides the energy for research, heightens my potential as a sense maker and means that research has relevance to my life as a whole, not just my conceptual knowing.

(1986: 194)

---

3 For example, in my research interviews I always end by asking the respondent how she found the experience. Frequently, in response to this or to other questions she will say, 'I hadn't seen it that way before' or 'Talking about it clarified ...'. This is equivalent to the aim and content of more overt therapeutic encounters.

A high level of personal commitment to research does not represent 'bias' but is in fact a vital part of any study, as Judi Marshall (1986) points out.

The study here is multi-layered and multi-dimensional. I did this research because I was interested in this area for several reasons. I wanted to obtain a Ph.D., but as soon as I began engaging with the respondents, from the time of setting up interviews, doing the interviews, transcribing and analysing them and returning to see the respondents again, that objective became only one of many. It was replaced at stages by more short-term considerations although the thought of thesis completion was ever-present, driving and enabling me to take a broader view of the subject matter of PND and the transition to motherhood.

Doing in-depth interviews meant that my involvement in these women's lives became suffused with emotion and anxiety connected with their lives but it was made all the greater for me on occasions by the overriding need to make something of the data for academic purposes. I had taken a risk in collecting qualitative data in this way. At the time I did so, there were almost no precedents, certainly not in social psychology and not for psychologists drawing upon sociological ideas.

Rowan (1981) describes effectively some of these anxieties of doing research and making sense of what comes out of it. He suggested that during the research process 'situations stir up anxieties and other feelings within the researcher, some of which may have much more to do with the researcher's own problems than anything going on out there in the world' (1981: 77). It is essential, then, not only to acknowledge but to explore one's personal 'action' as a researcher in order to understand the research processes and to recognise problems and anxieties which are related to this task and to attempt to predict any consequences. They are an integral part of the process at each stage.

As I got to know the women, I came to feel a sense of involvement and obligation for their well-being which was reinforced by comments about the value of my visits for letting off steam and unburdening themselves of certain anxieties. It was clearly an integral part of the research process for them, not an objective, detached data-collecting exercise. Although I wanted the data for my thesis, I had to make a reassessment of what the data actually were and thus to 'count in' the social process of constructing knowledge.

Constructing the research relationship

The decision to examine the importance of the research interview itself for the production of knowledge about post-natal depression arose during the process of analysing the in-depth tape-recorded interviews. While this study had an overall aim of examining women's accounts of their experiences and emotional reactions at various stages in the first six months after childbirth, it became clear that the relationship between the interviewer and respondent was a dynamic, developing one. Most respondents gave thought to what they would say at the next meeting during the times between, i.e. the process of being a respondent produced a long-term self-conscious reflexivity. Thus they engaged with the interviewer in

LIVERPOOL
JOHN MOORES UNIVERSITY
AVRIL ROBARTS LRC
TEL. 0151 231 4022

a complex reflexive process which had implications for the meaning and under-standing of the data and in turn for the meanings of the experience itself. It there-fore raised important theoretical issues about the way individuals attribute and reflect upon the meaning of experience and subjectivity-identity, i.e. the research interview is part of a process of knowledge production – about both *subjectivity* and the *substantive content of the interview*, in this case the meaning of PND for the woman herself and as a general term.

Three aspects of the research relationship are discussed here because they most directly emerged from examination of the data produced in this way.

1   The researcher–respondent interactions as a *dynamic social process*.
2   The related *production of subjectivity* as both 'I'/'me' (i.e. immediate conscious-ness/self as subject and reflexive consciousness/self as object) over the months of the interviews.
3   The influence of *knowledge-claims of experts* and popular versions of knowl-edge-claims upon the 'me' or reflexive consciousness, self as object and the objectification of subjectivity through the process of reflexivity in a cultural context. Specific to the substantive issues – motherhood and PND – is that pregnancy, childbirth and early motherhood reflect the roles and cultural norm-setting by scientists and clinicians in respect of women's lives.

Researcher–respondent interactions

The relationship between the two participants in the research process built up its own momentum, and the low attrition rate over the first three interviews in par-ticular indicated, as several stated, that the interviews themselves were somehow 'therapeutic'. Thus in this extract from an interview with Angela:

> I find it really helpful to talk, especially when I feel depressed and frus-trated. I said to my friend, 'My psychiatrist is coming tomorrow.' If you hadn't been coming I would have got depressed.
>
> (Angela, Interview 3, p. 1)

Talking to another person in this way also stimulated reflexivity over time. Being interviewed made Jane think of herself and the changes through the transition to motherhood in a way that she would not have done otherwise.

> I used to see my friend sit there and play bricks and imagine things with her two boys and I'd think, 'How boring.' I thought I would think the same thing when I had a baby. I thought it'd be the same as before. It's not. I've changed in that way. I enjoy this sitting and playing. To see her smiling and laughing and everything – it's different to how I thought in the beginning. You don't realise how much you've changed until you talk about it like this.
>
> (Jane, Interview 4, p. 8)

Also, anxieties about the way a woman felt about the baby, particularly in relation to 'bonding' (see Chapter 4), were made explicit to the interviewer in a way that might have been difficult in another context and to an intimate other.

> I remember having dreams that I was ignoring him and he was dying and I thought for a while that it was actually happening. I found that a bit peculiar. I didn't really want him. But gradually I got to know him and it all worked out.
>
> (Jerri, Interview 2, p. 3)

This meant that the research became, inevitably, a form of intervention (possibly similar to counselling; see Coyle and Wright, 1996) in that (a) it demanded a reflexive consciousness from both participants and (b) it enabled the expression of feelings and ideas in confidence without the fear of 'diagnosis' or upsetting others – such as the baby's father, or a close relative – by expressing anxieties or antagonism. At the end of each interview, the woman was asked to assess whether she had found it interesting, helpful or not and why. This sustained the reflexivity required of the respondent.

The production of subjectivity and reflexive consciousness over the months of the interviews

Both Mead (1934/67) and Lacan (1949) have suggested a model of self/subjectivity that is preceded by the social order. Subjectivity is structured through gaining entry into the social world by taking a place in the symbolic order. Although self/subjectivity is not wholly fixed in either author's version, Lacan stresses the production of subjectivity through discursive relations and the centrality of language in consciousness/self-awareness which is within the *terms set by pre-existing social relations and cultural values*. Lacan theorises subjectivity in a way which enables resistance to the inherent subordination of women (see Urwin, 1984) but leads to a conclusion that subjectivity cannot transcend the existing pattern of social and discursive relations.

Examining the transcripts revealed an ongoing dialogue which on the practical level was part of a 'getting to know' scenario through which the respondent managed her self-presentation to the interviewer. However, this was tied to discursive and unconscious levels of knowledge. In the extracts that follow there is evidence of the way the interview encourages relation of self to context and a dynamic reproduction of self through reflexivity. In A1 below, Angela uses reference points of conversations with others and her ongoing account of herself to me to focus on the contradictions of her changing self-consciousness (me/discursive consciousness) opposed to her I/subjective/practical consciousness. According to Giddens' theory there are also indicators of the unconscious present in her transcripts which represent the link between the contradictory facets of her subjectivity.

Thus she says: 'I can't understand why my memory is just going' (practical consciousness/I). She reflects upon why she is so concerned (i.e. her previous skills and her fear of being as her mother seems to be). She also talks of herself as having a 'lack of routine' – she is lost behind the children, she has lost her memory. She is actively becoming something she does not wish to be. Because she cannot explain these contradictions, she deals with them by saying: 'I think it's just me.'

A1

ANGELA: I was saying to my friend the other day, 'I can't understand why my memory is just going! It used to be so good.' I suppose it's because of the job I was doing. I'd remember numbers, faces, addresses – my memory was really spot on. And now, I'm just as bad as my mum, which is something I vowed I'd never ever be. It always used to annoy me when my mum was so forgetful. I remember getting very cross with her at times. Now I'm doing exactly the same thing.

PAULA: How does that make you feel?

ANGELA: Oh I get really cross. It really does make me cross. And I was always so organised – everything was in its place and now everything's haywire [*laughs*]. Although I've probably got a routine with the children – but that's with the kids – I've lost my own routine. I've not got one myself any more, and I was finding since I seen you last – everything seems so chaotic. I was finding myself still in my night-clothes at 2.00 in the afternoon. I used to find that dreadful. I used to get really fed up. I'd say to Mark 'For God's sake do something with those children – I want a bath – I just want to sit in the bath!' I found that instead of bathing three or four times a week it was going down to once. I was sometimes lucky if I got that in. I had to book an appointment so that I could have a bath. I was getting really down about that, but I'm beginning to get over that a bit now.

PAULA: So what got you over that stage?

ANGELA: I think it's just me. I've always been an up and down sort of person. One minute I can be very elated and then I go rock bottom. I sink very quickly. Mark says I'm very moody. I let things get on top of me which I shouldn't do. That's probably why. So I have to bring myself out – with his help.

(Interview 3, pages 9–11)

In extracts A2, A3 and A4, Angela again wavers between seeing herself as moody, or someone who is always in extreme moods. It is not clear to me, the observer, what she means. She has always expressed herself to me without showing any extremes of emotion, although she was well able to articulate her feelings from a distance. She is clear how her subjective/practical consciousness is constantly mediated both by what she believes others expect and the ways that she has accounted for herself both during the interview and reflexively during the progress of her biography. She has constructed herself for herself and others, but the current experience is placing that in some jeopardy so that the different levels of consciousness are simultaneously visible during the interview process.

A2

PAULA: Have you been depressed at all since I've seen you last?

ANGELA: Um. I'm a terribly moody person. No I'm wrong – I'm not moody. I can be very high or very low. Very rarely am I in the middle. Now I find it easier to handle the thought of being home – it doesn't worry me as much as it did before. I think some of it is what you think other people are expecting of you – that you should be out there doing your bit. But you're doing your bit in the house. But it doesn't worry me so much now. ... I do have big highs and big lows, but I've always been like that so I don't know if you can say it's related to having a baby or not.

Does post-natal depression come more the first time than the second? I think you're more content come the second one because you haven't got the anxieties that you do with the first one. You've accepted the situation. Mark said, 'Why don't you just not worry about a job until they're at school – because you'd be in a better frame of mind?'

But it wouldn't worry me if I stayed at home till they started school. I'd be happy just to poddle along like I am at the moment.

A lot of depression – well it's the money. If you've got financial worries, I don't think there's anything worse than that. It drags you down.

It's your own torment inside because when you do get money problems you think it would help if you did go back to work and get a job. This tossing ideas backwards and forwards. I know Mark worries about money. It doesn't bother him that I don't work. He doesn't let the money side of it get him down as much as it worries me.

When I get uptight with Carey and say, 'Kids, who'll have them?', he says, 'It's your choice', which is a typical male comment, but it's true, for men really are happy to go along with what a woman wants. It was my choice. I don't think he would have bothered if I had said that I didn't want any.

(Interview 4, pages 6–8)

A3

ANGELA: I have cried during this pregnancy. It's a bit strange. I've cried so much – I don't think there's much left in me.

PAULA: Would you describe yourself as depressed then?

ANGELA: No. I'm not depressed. I'm still worried about money. It's always in the back of my mind, but I wouldn't say I was depressed now. Mark thinks I am. He says, 'You get depressed at the drop of a hat.'

(Interview 1, page 17)

A4

PAULA: Do you think, looking back over the last three months, that you've changed much?

ANGELA: Yes. It's funny that you should say that because I've been trying to get back to work. I've got Mark home in the day, and there've been a few jobs going. I want to get back into typing – I don't want to waste my skills. I've got very resentful of being turned down because of my skills. I've got very resentful of being turned down because of having young children. Once it wasn't said to me, but another one said he was worried that I had young children. It annoys me that they won't even let you put your side of it.

I found it hard. I'm frightened I'm going to end up cleaning or stacking shelves in a supermarket because I know that's a job – but I want to use the skills I've got – I don't want to lose my typing.

It runs a close second that I need to go back to work to have another interest. I think I'd had a bad day recently. I was talking to my friend and said, 'When you become a housewife you virtually have an operation to have your brain removed. You just become like a vegetable.' I found it hard filling in forms – going back to schooldays about what qualifications I've got. For the first couple I found it hard to sit and think about things other than children and shopping lists. That I resent.

(Interview 3, pages 4–5)

In H1 Hilary is paying attention to her knowledge, built upon through her reflexive and discursive consciousness, using her unfolding biography as reference points. She has constructed a version of female professional behaviour, and understands herself in the *past* in relation to that. Women who cope well in a man's world deserve the confidence they develop. Thus the shift to the all-female world of the mother produces contradictions in subjective consciousness. Her expectation of competence as a professional woman, a crucial part of her identity, can only be transferred to competence at motherhood if she gives up the more valued part of herself (i.e. one who competes effectively with men).

H1

HILARY: I do think that most women I know have been much better in their jobs than the men I know. I don't think – perhaps that's unfair to men – but it's been my experience over a long period of time really. That's what I felt about me in the past. I was better than the men I knew. Maybe I'd made a big thing about that in the past, maybe I felt that I'd got confidence despite being a woman in a man's world. And being forced back into the woman's role, and actually finding it so stressful, exaggerated it. I think that was true. All of a sudden you're forced to being back with women. Having been out and feeling equal, free and confident, all of a sudden I was forced back into a woman's position. I didn't like it. I just couldn't cope. It didn't feel good and part of me did not want it to feel good. I thought, 'I don't want to be an expert at changing nappies.'

PAULA: The irony is that your relationship with your daughter is not prescribed by your ability to take her to the clinic and change nappies better than anyone else. But it is interesting how that takes over and people evaluate your mothering that way.

HILARY: I think it's being forced back into a woman – into the stereotype of a mother. That's what I found hard, and part of me wanting success and part of me felt I was OK in the career. And also I felt I had joined the women and needed to get points for what I was doing.

(Interview 1, pages 8–9)

In extract H2 below, taken from the third interview, she is clearly sinking into the subjective experiences that she feared. The interaction with individual health professionals and mothers is reinforcing her sense of self as an incompetent mother, and continuing to distance her from the competent professional self. She is attempting to bring the past, present and future of her biographical context into a discursive consciousness to make sense of her life.

H2

PAULA: So I want to ask you how you have been since I last saw you.

HILARY: Apart from needing to lose some weight I feel back to normal pretty well. That's quite nice. I go out on good mornings and feel quite normal. I'd just like to get to the spring and not eat so much. I keep telling myself I'm feeding the baby so it's alright to keep eating. But I'm quite worried about going back to work. I keep thinking, 'How am I going to organise all this and get up and so on?' But I'm sure I will in the end. But I think it's going to be a bit hectic. One of the nice things now is that I can have a fairly slow start to the day – it might be early – but I'm having breakfast for the second time at 9 o'clock and of course that won't be possible. I think it will be the first Monday in May. We've got a holiday at the end of May. They're very busy as usual. I'm just worried about coping really. I got used to the boring domestic routines which you suddenly think are important and aren't really.

(Interview 3, page 2)

The influence of knowledge-claims of mainstream clinical scientists

The way that knowledge-claims about women's psychology are structured, and the power of dominant social groupings employing vested interests to set norms and influence popular knowledge, are also crucial to understanding the genesis of research paradigms and human socialisation. The priority western society gives to science is more problematic in the late twentieth century than ever before.

Psychology relies for its data on the practices of socialised and culture-bound individuals, so that to explore 'natural' or 'culture-free' behaviour (i.e. that behaviour unfettered by culture, social structures and power relations) is by definition impossible, which is a state of affairs that normally goes unacknowledged. Socialisation is influenced by the press and broadcast media, which report scientific 'discoveries'. Individuals become so familiar with these that they are influenced in the way they assess their own behaviours in relation to the scientific 'norms'. They respond in ways that link their own sense of being to such norms and when these individuals themselves are the subjects of psychological research their relationship to the norms created by scientists are revealed in the findings and lend support to the original claims (see Nicolson, 1993, for further discussion of this argument). The interconnectedness of science, the media and gendered subjectivity therefore needs to be explored when assessing the validity and legitimacy of scientific knowledge-claims.

Women's accounts of their post-natal experience suggested that it was not a clinical condition – they explained themselves in the context of their own biographical experiences – but they sometimes related their experiences to popular clinical concepts. Here I examine this approach to understanding their experiences by returning to extracts from the data and interpreting them within a specific theoretical framework that emerged from the original analysis of the data set as well as a further dimension developed in subsequent analysis of reflexivity, interviewing and the process of long-term participation.

Three specific issues emerge. First, respondents, aware that I wanted to know about PND and having had post-natal experiences of being depressed, talk about PND spontaneously and distance themselves from it. Thus they develop *implicit theories of prevention*. Second, they distance themselves from the concept by employing *alternative terminologies*. Third, the respondents could perceive an experience as PND in retrospect while at the time looking at it in a different way – more from within (as subject) rather than from the outside (as object).

Implicit theories of prevention

The ideological constraints which merge motherhood and femaleness and which are apparent in the discursive and practical understandings of the experience of becoming and being a mother, for most women reflect received notions of the 'good mother'. Thus women understand themselves practically: do they suffer from post-natal depression or not? At the discursive level, a woman may realise her experience is not related to the baby–mother and childbirth experiences *per se* and thus make sense of her experiences in other ways, as in many of the extracts above.

The existence of the medical–clinical discourse serves to regulate the extent to which women perceive themselves as liable to 'fall foul' of such hazards. In other words, the tension between recognising the pathologising effect of being labelled as having 'post-natal depression' and *feeling* depressed generates an alternative set of explanatory accounts which emerge as subjective theories of prevention. The women in this study actively positioned themselves outside the 'blues' discourse: they understand the 'blues' as occurring for no rational reason, whereas their emotional reactions were all comprehensible to them. Similarly, although several respondents reported feeling very 'low' at times, everyone denied they had 'post-natal depression'. Only two women did not feel negative at all: one woman exchanged roles so that her partner stayed at home to look after the baby; another had a partner who worked part-time and took over the care when he arrived home. All the others reported some degree of negative feeling, but stressed the strategies they employed to avoid 'post-natal depression'. One coped

> because of the support I had at first. ... I feel for me that was the thing that made the difference because there was always someone to lift you out when things weren't going terribly well.
>
> (Ruth, Interview 3)

For another, a post-natal class and support group was the solution.

> The post-natal class was a terrific help. The girl who took the classes was really good. You went along – she's trained – something to do with children – it's gone, it's gone completely! She came into the hospital and she knew what she was talking about. I went to the post-natal classes and it was wonderful listening to other people's problems. There was always someone with a worse problem than you. I felt the post-natal class helped me tremendously. Not everyone does them. It was a great help to be able to talk about problems such as sore nipples, a routine, the day-to-day problems. For example, if you can't get out of the house you sit and think, 'My God I'm the only one with these problems.' If you can't talk about it to anyone it's a disaster. It's what starts dragging you down – which is where your post-natal depression might appear because you literally get depressed about everything.
>
> (Sharon, Interview 3)

Other women found it necessary to avoid monotony.

> ... sometimes I don't have to go to a certain place, but in my mind I make it that I have to go, so I get out. I go out nearly every day, and so the couple of days that I do stay in, I really enjoy it.
>
> (Natasha, Interview 2)

> It was background panic. I've felt that I haven't had time to get depressed. I'm alright as long as I'm busy and I see a lot of people. If I was in the house with just him and not seeing anyone, then I don't think it would be hard to get depressed.
>
> (Felicity, Interview 3)

However, the problem about keeping busy also had negative consequences.

> ... although I've got a routine with the kids I've lost my *own* routine. ... It's a terrible thing to admit, but I went for two days without even washing. I sat down and had a good cry and I said to Mark, 'This just isn't on because I'm really going to go down if I'm not careful.' And you think at the back of your mind, 'Oh God, am I suffering from depression?' And I think I can't be because I know what I'm doing and have to stop myself doing it.
>
> (Angela, Interview 3)

These extracts are indicative of a complex process stimulated by reflexivity demanded through participation in this project.

There were, however, attempts by some women to avoid the consequences of PND by denying that they had felt depressed.

> I had a bit of a depression while he [the baby] was in hospital – but it wasn't depression really. It wasn't what I'd call 'post-natal depression'. It was unhappiness that he had to go through it ... coming home from hospital and no baby. That churned me up a bit.
>
> (Adrienne, Interview 3)

Alternative terminology

This denial of being depressed also occurred through renaming the experience. The negative feelings and experiences are translated into a different set of terms from those employed within the medical–clinical discourse. I list them to demonstrate:

> I don't think I would describe it as feeling down or depressed but ... 'panicky'.
>
> (Ruth, Questionnaire at 6 months)

> I get fed up ... I just feel I'd like something more than just sitting at home.
>
> (Angela, Interview 4)

> I have times of being really fed up.
>
> (Shirley, Interview 4)

> Torment inside.
>
> (Angela, Interview 4)

> I feel it's just like mourning. There are things you have to go through.
>
> (Norma, Interview 4)

> I feel low, dreadfully low.
>
> (Penelope, Interview 2)

I feel low.

(Meg, Interview 3)

It just bugs me ... I'm stuck at home.

(Sharon, Interview 4)

The days drift through in a haze of half washing up. ... To a sort of extent I feel a physical drudge. ... I get very uptight.

(Sylvia, Interview 4)

I find I'm pre-occupied ... in a world of my own. My concentration has gone a bit.

(Samantha, Interview 3)

I didn't feel depressed – although I'd like to think that! Maybe I did – I don't know.

(Matilda, Interview 3)

I got through the so-called 'post-natal depression' time without being depressed – although I was upset a couple of times about specific things which I could say 'that's why I got upset'. But I didn't get 'post-natal depression'.

(Frances, Interview 2)

I feel supersensitive. ... It is usually triggered by something fairly rational. ... I feel fairly low and tired.

(Sarah, Interview 2)

I'm not depressed – just pissed off.

(Natasha, Interview 4)

I feel churned up generally.

(Sarah, Interview 3)

It seems, then, that the respondents are well aware of a popular aetiology of PND which they find alien to their experiences. Thus they need to rename and consequently distance themselves from PND and all they know about it.

Objectifying PND

The relationship of self to the context (social, biographical) needs to be related in some ways to perceived social norms – particularly during a life crisis. The transition to motherhood is one particularly informed by the medical/scientific discourse through which priority is given to explanations which pathologise women (see Chapter 4). Women are expected to be good mothers and take to the related roles and tasks with little difficulty. However, there is also an expectation that women hold that they might in fact suffer from PND. In order to contextualise their experiences outside this discourse, some employ a strategy that objectifies PND, treating it as a pathology, but one which is outside themselves.

In H3 we can see how Hilary sees language as directly prescribing the required style of behaviour for a good mother, and her inability or unwillingness to accept that makes her feel that she cannot match the norms of motherhood.

H3

PAULA: What do you think is success in mothering?

HILARY: I don't think there are criteria, but it's what people say to you. Like 'Oh she's very quiet you know' or 'Does she go through the night?' These are all things that are like sort of hurts. After a while you don't want to say anything as you're not sure what the right answer is. In a way you don't want to join the game. And there's this language I can't abide. 'Does she go down in the afternoon?' As if she's going down a well! No, I don't drop her anywhere. It's quite peculiar and a lot of the time I want to take the mickey really. But of course if the child isn't 'going down' you do worry: 'Oh dear me, I haven't done this right.' All I want is that we enjoy each other's company, and how that matches up with other people's ideas about what is good or what's a good child I don't know.

(Interview 1, page 9)

In S1, Sharon makes reference to the bonding discourse. While it is prevalent and pervasive in popular versions of the medical discourse concerned with the first hours of mothering (so much so that the idea has influenced the procedures of the maternity wards), women are confused about its meaning. Here Sharon appears to have assumed it means she is expected to feel and act as if permanently welded to her infant, and she punishes herself for feeling she wants to go out by asserting that she will not wean her son. It also looks as if the 'obvious answer' has come from others, possibly her husband, and that she is punishing him by opting for her understanding of the mother–infant bond and will neglect him as he has her.

S1

SHARON: I've often wondered about 'bonding'. I sat in hospital and waited for it to start. [*laughs*]

PAULA: Well I think it means a good relationship really.

SHARON: You do? I don't know. He's so much part of my life now that losing him would be ghastly. And looking back, we had a terrific life before, but looking back I can see what was missing. We had a great time before. And I'm a little resentful at the moment that we can't go skiing. And for example last night someone rang up and they had tickets for *Chess* tonight [a West End play at the time]. And Peter's going. That really did hurt. The obvious answer is wean him onto the bottle – but he's little for such a short time. I'm not going to do that. What does it matter if I can't go out? [*laughs*] I get very upset about it at times, but at other times I realise that it just doesn't matter at all. I'm not going to wean him.

(Interview 2, pages 4–5)

However, with Angela it is clear that, while she actively wants to distance herself from PND, which she dismisses, she would like to have such a label to explain her anxieties/depression later which she cannot find a label for. She does not seem to see her emotional reactions to parenting a difficult toddler as explicable, other than through her own pathology. Thus a label of PND would help her sense of self. Nevertheless, she is also obedient to the constraints of the clinical discourse.

A5

PAULA: Then you had Jeremy and became a little depressed after that?

ANGELA: Yes. Not straight away. That's why I'm interested in the idea of post-natal depression. I remember when I was pregnant, people said you could get this depression. When you've had the baby you do get tearful, but I don't think that is post-natal depression – that's just hormone unbalance and the trauma your body's just gone through. It takes time before your body gets back to normal again. But more came out about a year later – and I think that's perhaps that people should say it doesn't happen straight after the baby's born, because you've got such a gap. You think you're all right, and it's got nothing to do with the baby because that was a year ago. But it must be.

PAULA: Did you find a baby of that age difficult?

ANGELA: No. I don't think so because I find him difficult now [aged 2]. I think that 18 months to two years is a bad time, and being pregnant [i.e. with another child] doesn't help because you haven't the energy. He wasn't particularly difficult at a year. It was just me. The depression was not really related to Matthew – it just came out. I felt so stupid. I thought Mark [husband] didn't find me attractive any more, so it's still to do with me.

PAULA: Where do you think those feelings come from?

ANGELA: I don't know. But I can remember talking about this the other day. I said, 'Do you remember what I was like?' and he said, 'I remember that you'd jump at the slightest thing, and your temper was really short.' But he didn't remember me having a go at him all the time.

(Interview 1, pages 13–14)

Knowledge of subjectivity and PND is discursive. That is, there is no objective means of identifying self (say through personality questionnaires/inventories) and there is no objective means of identifying PND. The research interview which takes account of changes over a period of crisis, as with the transition to motherhood, demands a reflexivity from the respondent and researcher. This engages with the respondents' biographical context, particularly the way they account for themselves. Biography goes through a change with the transition to motherhood, and different levels of consciousness are witnessed through the research interview; the attempts to reconcile the sense of self as subject and as object of reflection continue over the time of the interviews.

The transition to motherhood particularly requires respondents to reflect upon the wider context in which women's roles are focused and upon the family. Thus they also experience the impact of the knowledge-claims of science which, while apparently contrary to their subjective experience/practical consciousness, become gradually reconciled with the sense of self as they accept their new experiences.

Conclusions

The evidence from these data suggests an intriguing relationship between the process of subjective accounting for a psychosocial transition over a sustained period, and power relations as represented by the medical/clinical discourse. Despite criticism of medical control over the 'natural' experience of becoming a mother (Kitzinger, 1975; Oakley, 1980) and evidence that medical and maternal accounts of what is important differ (Graham and Oakley, 1981), childbirth is a medical event in both the USA and the UK, and medical and surgical interventions are increasingly common during labour and delivery. The power of clinicians extends beyond the control of childbirth *per se*, and the post-natal depression discourse provides an excellent example of how norms are set for women's psychological experience of becoming a mother despite contradictions about the 'nature' and 'cause' of 'post-natal depression' (see Foucault, 1977). The post-natal depression discourse presents early motherhood as potentially problematic in a clinical sense rather than in practical, rational terms (see Dalton, 1980, quoted in Chapter 3) and this medical/clinical discourse regulates women's own accounting of their experience.

The sudden impact of childbirth and hospitalisation enables women to respond to any negative emotions and periods of depression in an immediate rather than reflexive manner: they appear to be taken unawares and their feelings are attributed to the rational consequence of negative experience. Their subsequent sustained engagement with the medically controlled transition to motherhood (post-natal care), and the research process through which they are encouraged to reflect upon the transition to motherhood, require them to account in a more considered way for their emotions to gain some distance, or to reposition themselves in relation to the dominant discourse. There are complex reasons for this that transcend the relationship between becoming a mother and the medical/clinical discourse. Foucault (1980) asserts that the most powerful discourses in a society determine what it is appropriate to think and discuss, so that whatever the individual defines as knowledge becomes subordinated to the dominant discourse. The medical discourse is a powerful one, reflecting the patriarchal value system.

Here, I have explored the ways in which self-conscious reflexivity stimulated by research both illuminates the power of dominant discursive practices and identifies the ways in which individuals attempt to reposition themselves according to their own experiences. This is particularly salient in the case of women whose psychology is defined by the dominant patriarchal value system. Women's subjective accounts are regulated by and subordinated to the dominant, culturally valued discursive practices so that respondents in this study were unable to validate their own accounts as contradictions of the superordinate discourse.

6

LOSS, HAPPINESS AND POST-NATAL DEPRESSION
The ultimate paradox

Introduction

This chapter explores the meaning of the transition to motherhood and the post-natal experience for the respondents. It specifically focuses upon emotions, responses and behaviour that could be identified as depression and thus *post-natal depression*.

It further outlines how far individual experiences of depression following child-birth could be linked to those experienced by others by confronting crucial questions. Are there common features of PND? Is PND related to the birth *per se*? Or is the woman's life and the meaning she placed upon that particular period of time more important in determining her emotional state? How far may any experience of depression in the post-natal period be assessed as either pathological or a reasonable response to specific stresses and pressures? The interview data are used to address these issues.

Loss and change

Hart (1976), following Glaser and Strauss (1971), argued that identity and status (i.e. social position linked to a role and set of social relationships) are bound together in such a way that status changes occurring at any stage throughout the life cycle potentially involve a shift or reinterpretation of progressively larger amounts of accumulated personal data and can constitute a critical phase for individual identity. The ultimate significance of the status change relates to the importance of the status being lost or acquired, the extent to which it interconnects with other constituent statuses and the level of expectation that surrounds the transition which may have already been partially incorporated into the self (Hart, 1976: 11).

The conceptualisation of the transition to motherhood is different from other status changes. 'Mother' is incorporated into a woman's identity from a very early stage. This may be true of a number of other status positions, such as 'adult', which are inevitable while 'mother' is not. The status position and associated behaviours of motherhood totally define a woman regardless of the details of her experience of becoming a mother. Paradoxically, becoming a mother (on each occasion) represents both a desired move to a status which gains a woman a recognised social position and identity, while it involves disruption and loss of her former status. The status passage from mother of one to mother of more than one child strengthens the role of 'mother' but also strengthens the loss of the former self and independence and control over life.

Loss

Hart (1976) has argued, in relation to divorce and status change, that 'the life associated with the old status may never be completely discarded' (1976: 104), with the first childbirth the old status of non-mother is annihilated because of the central importance of 'mother' in relation to female identity and the ideological symmetry between 'woman' and 'mother'. This makes it more difficult for women to experience the loss of their old self in a way conducive to their peace of mind. *They are not permitted to grieve or mourn*, as with other change. If they do they are pathologised. So strong is the taboo that women themselves frequently fail to admit their sense of loss in a conscious way.

In women's accounts of the post-natal months, they explain their experiences in terms which relate more closely to accounts of depression following hospitalisation (Revans, 1968), psychosocial transitions (Murray Parkes, 1971) and disruption and loss (Marris, 1986) than they do to those encapsulated in the clinical/medical discourse.

A critical theme in all the women's accounts over the time of this research was that of *loss*, which is taboo in the expert literature on birth and motherhood. The linking of 'loss' with childbirth also conflicts with everyday understanding of the transition to motherhood – the archetypal 'happy event'. Loss and motherhood then appear paradoxical. Of course they are not.

Women who become mothers (each time) lose at least their autonomy, sense of identity, work, time, friends, relationship pattern, sexuality, sense of their own body and health and comfort. These losses occur (like all such losses) in a complex way as part of biographical experience and in the context of subjective understanding.

There was a widespread acceptance that motherhood also meant a loss of autonomous identity. Most women felt that being a mother affected their personalities and that they were no longer independent and responsible for just themselves. However, they also found it difficult to see themselves as mothers.

The losses are not permanent but are the first stage of the transitional *change*. Matilda, Melanie and Jerri all specifically expressed the view that becoming a mother made them feel that they were 'growing' as people. Nevertheless, they acknowledged that it often took time to meet the new challenges that this altered status brought. First-time mothers appeared to experience the changes as more significant than those who were mothers already. However, as Meg (having her third baby) said, this new baby also represented a significant change because it eliminated any time that she and her husband could spend together, and she had some concern that she could see parenthood stretching ahead for another eighteen years.

Time to oneself and time to do things other than for the family was a major issue in the early days and months of motherhood. Hilary found it difficult to talk about herself as a separate being and did not expect to have any of her own time.

> I've readjusted what I consider time to myself. I supposed I've lowered my definition of what that really means.
>
> (Interview 3)

Felicity realised that

> it takes monumental powers of organisation in order to actually do anything ... time just disappears. ... It's all more consuming than I expected. I was unprepared for the fact that you can't do anything else, but I haven't resented that. I've quite enjoyed it in lots of ways.
>
> (Interview 2)

Loss of autonomy and time conspired, along with physical strain and exhaustion, to provoke a sense that a woman had lost her former appearance. Several respondents were concerned that their appearance had changed. Wendy remarked:

> I think I look an awful lot older than I did one year ago. I'm not worried about it, but it does concern me. I don't want to look gaunt and haggard.
>
> (Interview 3)

She felt she often smelled of 'baby' and was worried about this. Similarly, at six months after the birth Isobel said:

> I suppose I feel less feminine – more matronly, or womanly in some way that is hard to express. I definitely feel different about myself ... I know I'm not as young looking. I know I'm not the same shape as I used to be.
>
> (Interview 4)

Jane found

> I don't bother with myself as much as I did. Sometimes that gets me down – toe nails, hair and so on. But it's not always that bad because sometimes she'll lay on the floor and I can get my hair done.
>
> (Interview 4)

At five weeks post-partum Frances was

> longing to be thin again. The last part comes when you stop breast-feeding. I want to be nice and flat again.
>
> (Interview 3)

And Dion had anticipated it would be

> a nice relief to be thin and get rid of that big stomach … but I keep
> thinking, 'God, no shorts this year!'
>
> (Dion, Interview 1)

Samantha, who had become quite big in the latter stages of pregnancy, had lost
weight by twelve weeks, but had been a bit down when she tried to buy some
clothes and was still too heavy to fit into those she wanted. Penelope, who had been
so pleased about her weight reduction prior to pregnancy, had put on two stone
more than she had wanted to while she was pregnant and was very unhappy about
this. Angela too became very depressed by her weight gain. Sarah had started
aerobic classes by the time her baby was three months old and Wendy had started
jogging and swimming by that stage – both being concerned to return to pre-
pregnancy body sizes.

Some women were concerned about their body shape because of their sense of
self that had changed, and others were concerned because they were afraid of
losing their partner's affection. Disentangling motives about appearance is a complex
process.

The losses detailed so far all contribute to the sense that femininity and sexuality have been lost. To give birth and breast-feed a baby means that a woman
has to experience her body in a different way from being a sexual and sexually
attractive being. The body functions differently and the sensations are different.
Sometimes this is because of damage. For example, Sarah had difficulties
with sexual intercourse because of scar tissue. Other women such as Ruth and
Frances had problems with their breasts which included engorgement, infection
and sore nipples. It often takes up to twelve months before a woman feels
sexual after childbirth (see Alder, 1994). In addition, feeling feminine and good
about one's self, which corresponds with positive sexual feelings, changes over the
transition to motherhood. Becoming a mother meant becoming womanly rather
than feminine:

> I suppose I feel less feminine – more matronly or womanly in some way
> that's hard to express. I definitely feel different about myself … maybe
> the way I look at things and feel about myself. I know I'm not as young-
> looking. I know I'm not the same shape as I used to be.
>
> (Isobel)

Many respondents reported a loss of occupational identity, i.e. anything outside
the home the women were doing before this baby was born. There were a variety
of responses to the loss of occupational identity. Matilda, a student whose baby
was born during the summer vacation, found the autumn term stressful and did
not know whether she was like the other students any more. This remained true
when the baby returned to Africa with Matilda's mother during this time at the age

of three months theoretically to enable her to carry on and finish her degree course. However, she felt it became a different experience anyway.

Both Angela and Meg had ambivalent feelings towards their occupational identity. For Meg, a trained maths teacher, this baby arrived just before her intended return to teaching. She felt that the pregnancy was one of the biggest mistakes she had made.

> I had spent eight years being a mum and wanted to do something else. I'd just started supply teaching.
>
> (Interview 1)

However, six months before the baby was born, despite an earlier declaration that mothers with babies should not work, she began filling in applications for part-time supply teaching posts.

Angela had lost her occupational identity before she became a mother for the first time. She had left the police for secretarial work. After her second baby she applied for secretarial work because she was short of money and bored, but was unsuccessful, which brought about a great deal of distress (see Chapter 5).

Eight women permanently left work to have their babies and remain as full-time mothers. Natasha and Jane both experienced deteriorating relationships with their partners after the birth and missed work for the companionship it provided. However, they did not feel supported enough at home to apply for work during the period I was in contact with them.

Gwen, Sylvia, Jerri and Sharon all intended to remain at home until their families were in school, and all planned further children in the short term. Sylvia expressed uneasiness at not having her own income and all missed the companionship of colleagues. Jerri eventually did work on her husband's business accounts and appeared content with that.

Lynn's case was different in that her occupational role had disappeared with local government reorganisation, but she did do some consultancy and public speaking. That role she believed enhanced her life and enabled her to avoid depression potentially precipitated by the loss of her former post rather than the arrival of the baby.

Ruth was the exception to this subgroup in that work posed an excruciating dilemma for her. She left her lecturing post, which was stressful and involved her in a great deal of travelling. However, out of the blue she was offered a local part-time post. This led her to feel

> panicky. When I came to interview the people for the job of nanny, there were a couple of days when I felt I couldn't cope.
>
> (Questionnaire)

When she did find someone, she declared:

91

> I feel happier now but for a weekend it [returning to work] seemed like the biggest decision I had made in my life.
>
> (Questionnaire)

Several women who had decided to take maternity leave experienced similar dilemmas. Norma and Felicity were very anxious about working with a young baby. Isobel and Felicity were both expected to return full-time although intended to try to negotiate part-time work. Norma and Sarah both had the option of part-time work.

Isobel had formerly been very conscious of her professional status but at the fourth interview she felt:

> I'll never be able to cope with getting up at six o'clock every morning. Beforehand I used to tumble out of bed at eight and out of the door at five past! But I've got to be a bit more organised than that. As soon as I get home it's going to be bath time. Then we've got to start to think about meals and all sorts of things. Thinking about it more positively, I can cope with that aspect. What worries me is the baby.
>
> (Interview 3)

Sarah, also a professional, had thoughts of work looming which bothered her. At three months, though, she began to see work as possible once again. At six months, once she had begun to work part-time, she felt ambivalent about her work because of guilt feelings.

Felicity could not decide whether she wanted to return or not. She felt she'd done 'everything in the house I could be bothered with. But I really want to be back at work.' However, she also admitted she was 'daunted by the prospect' and 'unsure about how much stress I'll be under'.

Norma was terrified and angry about returning, partly because she did not like midwifery and had planned to leave and retrain as a health visitor before she discovered she was pregnant. However, once she had found a child minder and found she could work the hours of her choice she said:

> I am really happy. It worked out so well. It just shows you. I had built all this up ...
>
> (Interview 4)

She had felt, prior to that, that she might not be able to pick up her life again until her son started school.

For Melanie, the return to work presented no practical problems, as John had been the one to give up work. However, she felt she had little time to think about it because she returned from maternity leave after three months. When she did return to work, though, she felt nothing much had changed.

Shirley (who had taken six months' leave) was keen to return to her career, which remained central to her life. This was so much the case that:

I'm not prepared to make the sacrifices you need to make if you have more than one child.

(Interview 3)

By the fourth interview she declared herself ready to return because

I don't think I can take it any further. Although the six months has been interesting and everything else, you get the feeling that she needs to expand her horizons – and to be a child by herself. In my lifestyle you don't see much of other kids so [the nanny share] will be good for her.

(Interview 4)

Occupational identity was for all in various ways an important part of their sense of who they were. This loss was a loss of how they had experienced their lives before the baby, as successful and independent, as in Hilary's case (see the detailed extract in Chapter 5, pp. 78–9); it might have been that the work did not mean the same any more or simply there might have been the feeling that they once had a job and friends which they no longer had.

Having a baby is marked by a series of complex losses in women's lives alongside the gain of the baby and status as mother. Women are actively prevented from mourning their losses because of social constraints and the unconscious acceptance of those constraints. Marris (1986) had argued that grieving is a 'process of psychological re-integration, impelled by the contradictory desires at once to search for and recover the lost relationships and to escape from painful reminders of loss' (1986: vii). For mothers the contradictions are more apparent in that the reminder of loss of an autonomous self (i.e. the baby) is constantly present and also, as they get to know the baby more, it increasingly becomes the focus of attachment and love (see Sluckin et al., 1983). Marris' research in a variety of social situations (widowhood, rehousing, pioneering new businesses) led him to identity unifying features. Central is that the anxieties associated with change are centred upon the struggle to defend or recover a meaningful pattern of relationships. While he does not include childbirth, he draws attention to 'A characteristic ambivalence, which I first noticed in the reactions of the bereaved, [which] seemed always to inhibit any straightforward adjustment' (1986: 1). This, Marris suggests, is because resistance to change is a fundamental feature of human psychology. In order to adapt to loss and change we have to have the ability to *protect* the assumptions of experience as well as reconsider them. The continuing viability of a structure of meaning in the face of new kinds of experience 'depends on whether we can formulate its principles in terms abstract enough to apply to any event we encounter, or ... ignore or prevent experiences which could not be comprehended in terms of it' (1986: 17). Thus an inherent psychological impulse to conservatism insists on the need for *continuity* of experience. When an essential thread is broken, individuals struggle to repair it – both seeking and resisting change. So a woman (and possibly her partner) might seek to have a baby and accordingly change her life. But this means disruption of her experience of continuity. A grieving process as a means of psychological reintegration is denied under the ideological conditions of the transition to motherhood and is labelled as pathology.

Change

Loss, however, does eventually lead to reintegration and change for most people. This is notable in the third and fourth interviews, where some expressions of a deep level of change were clearly present.

The ways in which women changed depended very much on their personal experiences, biographical context, events surrounding the birth and early post-natal months. Frances felt split between the two children, her husband and trying to make time for herself, something which Hilary dismissed as impossible. Others, for example Isobel and Natasha, felt 'older' but not in a particularly positive way. Norma, however, expressed the view that she could separate herself from some of the pettiness of her former life and in certain ways saw some of her friends as immature, which she had not done before. Sarah said that being a mother has

> made me feel much more adult. I always felt not properly grown up. ... I always felt as if I'd been a daughter, and a little daughter until I had a family of my own and then I could be an adult daughter.
>
> (Interview 3)

Melanie felt the baby made her more contented.

> I think I'm much happier than I was before. It's a difficult thing to put into words. But I think I'm more content. I feel 'rounded off'.

Jerri felt that she no longer had to prove herself to others any more:

> Now I couldn't care less what they think of me.
>
> (Interview 4)

Having the baby gave her that extra edge of confidence. She said that she felt more 'herself'.

Becoming a mother may enable a greater sense of maturity.

> I feel more separate from my parents. I feel I have joined a 'secret club' of women who have children.
>
> (Sarah)

Sometimes it is only having a second baby that brings this feeling:

94

You feel more of a mother. More at ease. More complete.

(Angela)

However, it was not necessarily the case that achieving motherhood and a greater sense of maturity or adulthood made someone more secure in their identity.

In theory I'm the same. In practice I'm probably slightly less confident than I thought I'd be. ... I've changed very little – perhaps I feel a little more grown up now.

(Frances)

Nevertheless, some women do experience some sense of psychological *fulfilment* which is unmistakable and directly connected to motherhood.

Fundamentally there is something about being a mum that is quite magical really. ... You can say it's love, motherhood or whatever!

(Meg)

Matilda felt

maybe for a long time or for the first time in my life I'm extremely confident in myself ... it's as if I'm sending some sort of waves to people to say, 'Look at me – what I am now.' They sense the feeling that I'm a lot more stronger than before.

(Interview 3)

The myth of the new man

Despite the positive view that most of the respondents had had about their partners prior to the birth, there were many ways in which they felt let down by them. Jane's case is typical. She told of a difficult day when she was exhausted because the baby had been particularly tired and irritable. Her fiancé went out for a drink with his friends and did not return until four in the morning. That was the first time. After that he frequently went out and came home very late, saying that he did not think that the baby should change his life.

More subtly, Frances' husband told her she was not a good mother, a role in life she would not have chosen if it had not been for his insistence. He was very good at handling the children and criticised the way she coped with them. This eroded her confidence, which had diminished anyway since the birth of the second baby.

In Matilda's case her husband had been abroad and not returned until several weeks after the birth. She felt very angry with him because of this although she felt guilty about doing so.

I felt very proud that I'd managed on my own without him at all. On the other hand, whenever she cried I tended to 'throw her' in his direction and say, 'Change her!' He thinks I'm just nagging him.

(Interview 3)

Shirley's partner slowly withdrew from his original promise to look after the baby. She felt overall he was generally supportive, but his share of the tasks diminished in the course of the six months after the birth.

I think if Mike and I have arguments it will be about Anna ... probably I'll get more irritated if he doesn't take an interest.

(Interview 3)

Isobel found that, although her husband was very enthusiastic and helpful at first, supporting her when she needed it, after about two months she could no longer cope because he had opted out. The baby cried a great deal and neither of them had much sleep.

There was obviously a lot of tension building up in my husband and if either of us has had post-natal depression it was him!

(Interview 3)

He became hostile towards her as he became more sleep-deprived and tense and was eventually arrested for drunken driving and prescribed anti-depressants. This in turn made her feel depressed and trapped.

Wendy's husband invited his brother to stay with them shortly after she arrived home:

they're both out at work and I cook the evening meal. And they just sit around drinking coffee and talking in the evenings. They don't help with the washing up or anything like that. I was thinking, 'Should I carry on feeling resentful or should I do something?'

(Interview 2)

She later declared that she had totally lost her faith in men.

Penelope's partner was in France on holiday when the baby was born. He returned home a few hours before she was discharged from hospital.

I was so angry with him. I hated him. I felt he had let me down totally, and he said he'd write or phone and we'd just had one postcard and I didn't know where the hell he was. And it was the fact that I couldn't discuss anything with anyone over the decisions I was trying to make. I was going batty. It was just dreadful and I felt totally isolated.

When we got home I knew I couldn't cope with the cats. Some friends did a clean up because Roger had left the place in chaos. Another friend made tea and gave me flowers. Roger came in at lunch time.

(Interview 3)

She reported that he was unsupportive to her throughout the time I interviewed her. He did not see why his night's sleep should be disrupted and did not appear to help Penelope recover from her ordeal. At the last interview (which was nine months after the birth) his behaviour was slightly better, but Penelope burst into tears when she told me that she could never forgive him for letting her down as badly as he had done.

At the final interview Isobel felt that her husband had never put the baby before himself as she had done.

> I've got to retrain him. He was fantastic to start with, then he probably started thinking I'm here all day so it was probably my job to look after the baby. And if a nappy needs changing he'll say to me, 'I think a nappy needs changing.'
>
> (Interview 4)

Natasha's partner was also apparently uncommitted to giving her support. At first he played with the baby but after a few weeks he started going out, which made her feel very low in spirits. This situation got worse and by six months she was really fed up because she was stuck at home while he could go out for a drink straight from work and she did not know when to expect him home.

> I may be silly but sometimes I think he just wants me to be stuck in all day. His life hasn't changed. He's got to do overtime, but I think 'anything to get out of the house and he's happy!'
>
> (Interview 4)

At the time of the last interview he rarely played with the baby, told her he was unsure whether their marriage had been a good idea because she was so possessive and he would not baby-sit to allow her to go out or be alone even for short periods. Sylvia found her husband 'thrilled' over the baby but not supportive of her.

> He sort of accepts that I'm ratty and tired because I don't get a chance to rest or do anything. He doesn't do anything positive to counter it. Occasionally he does. Eventually he'll say, 'Well I'll prepare supper' rather than 'Don't worry about supper I'll prepare it'. In other words he'll say, 'Do you want me to prepare supper?' if it looks as if he's not going to get his dinner!
>
> (Interview 2)

Meg's husband looked after the children while she was ill, but more or less stopped doing anything once she had recovered. He did, however, encourage her to nap at weekends.

> ... the interesting thing about Brian is the couple of times I've been out and left him with the baby he's jibbed at changing the nappies. Last night I said, 'Look there he is. I've cleaned his bottom, there's a nappy, put it on. Then I'll give you something to eat.'

(Interview 3)

Very few of the fathers met their partners' expectations in relation to emotional support and child-care, which in certain cases (such as Penelope and Isobel) was a significant factor in making the women depressed and anxious (Nicolson, 1990).

Conclusions

Motherhood is tough. Pregnancy, labour and the early post-natal weeks are times of extreme change in physiology, body size, function and shape. The birth of a baby is shocking, painful, physically damaging and leads to anxiety, distress and an important sense of responsibility. It is also pleasurable and magical. The first months of motherhood (each time) require major shifts in relationship patterns and work (domestic and occupation) while the mother is recovering from the aftermath of the birth. There is little doubt and should be no surprise that this transition is likely to lead to mood and emotional lability.

Women's lives and the gains, losses and mechanisms of psychological change and development are dependent upon biography and individual experience and meaning as a function of that biography. However, there is also strong evidence that women having babies have much in common.

Post-natal depression is not pathological. It probably should be considered the rule rather than the exception. It is also potentially a healthy, grieving reaction to loss. However, in the current framework, the image of the happy, healthy and energetic new mother maintains its hold on the public imagination and thus depression remains a case for treatment.

7

KNOWLEDGE, MYTH AND THE MEANING OF POST-NATAL DEPRESSION

... it has been consistently communicated to women that their moods and feelings ... are hormonally controlled.

(Choi, 1994: 128)

Midwives have seen the consequences of allowing obstetric definitions of pregnancy and birth to dominate maternal care. New motherhood, traditionally the business of the community and of experienced women, has entered the 'professional' domain where psychologists, social workers, psychiatrists, child health nurses, midwives, obstetricians and paediatricians all have a vested interest. This professional involvement appears to be resulting in a pathologizing of processes which are social rather than medical.

(Barclay and Lloyd, 1996: 138)

Introduction

Women are seen as the victims of their bodies, particularly the raging hormones that plague their lives from adolescence to late middle age. Science, clinical experts and popular myths portray women as emotionally and intellectually unreliable, unpredictable, deficient and a psychological puzzle – all because, for some of their adulthood, they have the capacity to ovulate (Caplan and Caplan, 1994; Gannon, 1994). Post-natal depression is part of that belief system. For centuries women have been dying from childbirth and experiencing severe ill-health caused by the stresses and strains of motherhood (Shorter, 1984). So why is depression in the weeks and months following birth perceived as 'atypical' (Nicolson, 1992a; Ussher, 1991)? Women's capacity and determination to bear and nurture children under adversity seems endless; but it is not their resilience that interests scientists and clinicians. It is their failure.

So what contribution has research made to understanding the psychological consequences of becoming a mother? Traditionally motivated research and interest in PND flourished during the 1990s (see Chapters 2 and 3). Here I examine the purpose, processes and consequences of this expansion *for women*. Has it improved understanding and opportunities for more effective health care? Are scientists nearer to answering the question 'What is post-natal depression'? Have researchers taken account of feminist challenges to the concept of PND and the blaming of women's bodies to re-evaluate their findings and adapt methodology? It seems that the answer to all these questions is no (Jelabi, 1993; Barclay and Lloyd, 1996). The greater the interest in PND the more 'cases' are identified but little is done to enable the women to cope with their domestic and child-care responsibilities. In fact, some of the interest in PND has a direct negative conse-quence on women's emotional lives. That is that since the end of the 1980s re-search questions about the impact of maternal depression on infant and child well-being have proliferated. This 'mother blaming' is not new, of course. Since the work of Freud and Bowlby on maternal deprivation (see Chapter 1), there has been a social focus upon women's role as mothers. The formation of a secure attachment between mother and child has been related to outcomes in mental health throughout that child's life. While the maternal deprivation thesis has un-dermined women's confidence in their parental abilities if they worked outside the home and subtly forced them back there, the negative consequences for the child of their mothers being depressed because they *were at home* can only be solved if the mothers are deemed *pathologised* and *treated*. Here the mother's state of mind is not only positioned as the curse of family life because she is depressed and irritable, but the mother in this case is *dangerous* (see Chapter 1). But why do we take such evidence seriously? It seems that whatever the research question and whatever research findings emerge women cannot win. Perhaps there is some-thing wrong with women's bodies and minds if these are consistent scientific findings?

PND and the construction of knowledge

But how do we come to *know* what we think we know about PND? All knowledge is problematic, although some forms of knowledge appear to be endowed with greater credibility than others. As Foucault asserts, knowledge is *political*. In order to understand where knowledge is 'coming from' and the way it is used, vested interests need to be identified and the spheres of influence of those making the claims to knowledge exposed (Foucault, 1980; Ussher, 1991; Chapter 3).

The knowledge of PND that is given priority in terms of stating the 'truth' which influences health-care policy and clinical practice is based upon 'science' defined within narrow parameters (see Chapter 2). This science generally involves large-scale research, standardised instruments to enable comparison, control groups, random or representative sampling frames and an unquestioning assumption of the underlying concept of PND. There is no problem with this provided, as with all *good* science, the research is designed to answer specific questions and does not in itself make claims for its findings beyond the answers to those questions (see Oakley, 1990).

As with much of the research described in Chapters 2 and 3, such mis-representative extrapolation does not happen 'naturally'. The confluence of patriarchal knowledge-claims based on traditional research undoubtedly serves the vested interests of those who want to position PND as a *problem of* (rather than seek a *solution for*) women. In other words, women depressed after birth and in the early months of motherhood are pathologised. As Jane Ussher (1992) contends, this process underlies a broader and pervasive scientific discourse on women's bodies:

> Pregnancy, childbirth and the postnatal period have been pathologised in the same (convenient) way, positioning women's experiences as an illness in need of intervention, and interpreting any distress or unhappiness as individual pathology. Since the male obstetricians wrested control of childbirth from the women midwives as early as the sixteenth century childbirth has been construed as a technological accomplishment on the part of the expert – the woman herself positioned as a passive recipient, the ubiquitous stirrups in which she was trapped helpless and splayed, symbolising her position as a vessel to be relieved of its burden.
>
> (Ussher, 1992: 47–8)

If childbirth is a scientific, technical process accomplished by medical clinicians, there is little wonder that women are expected to be happy and grateful for the delivery of a healthy baby. Women's bodies are universally seen through the patriarchal telescope as the *other*. Traditional scientific approaches to PND imply incomprehension of maternal unhappiness, anxiety or depression. Motherhood is joyous, happy and fulfilling. Normal, healthy, feminine women do not respond negatively to motherhood. If they do there is something wrong with *them*. PND is *not* seen as a normal, potentially healthy response to severe disruption, loss and change. However, most people take these patriarchal myths seriously. This includes women and men, feminist and non-feminist. We all experience patriarchal knowledge as 'truth' in the first instance.

Traditional research deliberately and systematically denies the value of *women's experience* of the transition to motherhood. Evidence which takes women's accounts seriously and suggests PND to be other than pathological is dismissed as subjective and anecdotal. Somehow, because they are 'other', the context of women's lives is not a legitimate consideration for science.

The consequence of this is that only patriarchal knowledge feeds into policy, clinical practice and everyday understanding (see Chapter 5). Women's experiences of childbirth and the transition to motherhood are assigned to the margins of knowledge. Although increasing numbers of 'anecdotes' about women's experience are available through accounts in newspapers and magazines, their value is recognised only by women themselves and feminist professionals such as clinical psychologists, midwives and health visitors (e.g. Hoeft, 1994; Barclay and Lloyd, 1996). Such data do not serve the needs of scientists seeking for the measurable, objectively identifiable 'truth'. Hierarchies of knowledge are structured so that some forms 'count' and other forms are dismissed.

This process prioritises patriarchal perspectives. Jane Ussher argues that women should not perpetuate this silence about their experiences. Feminist researchers and theoreticians need to 'unveil the body as it is framed in the male gaze and reclaim it as our own' (Ussher, 1992: 56). Also, 'We are taught that our bodies are weak; that our bodies make us mad. Is it any wonder, then, that we turn to our bodies and to reproduction as a source of attribution when we *feel* mad?' (Ussher, 1991: 253). It is vital, then, to look at the processes of research as well as the ideology underlying research rationale and results. In Chapter 5 I argued that the interaction between the respondent and inter-viewer throughout the research process needs to be recognised as part of the knowledge base. One of the central driving elements in feminist research is to assert the importance of gender in making sense of evidence. Who carries out the research? Who reads it? Who (if anyone) applies it? All of these questions are alien within traditional paradigm but crucial for understanding the structure of power underlying data and claims made for them. Jonathan Smith (1992) acknowledges that being a man interviewing women through the transition to motherhood potentially constrains and even profoundly influences what is produced as data. The mothers he spoke to portrayed their pregnancy and birth differently from accounts they gave to women researchers in this area (see Oakley, 1981).

Knowledge is discursive, contradictory and problematic. It is based on vested interests, but not only the vested interests of scientists themselves (although for the most part it is they who have the power) but respondents also make some *choice* as to their self-presentation. Sandra Elliot (1994) has shown in a discussion of a screening programme for PND using the Edinburgh Postnatal Depression Scale (EPDS) that:

> It is important to realise, though, that the person administering the forms can influence the extent to which this happens by the manner in which they present the questionnaire and its purpose. For example, in a de-prived area of Stoke [a small industrial town in the English midlands], word got around that you shouldn't score high on that questionnaire or you'll get the health visitor turning up every week!
>
> (Elliot, 1994: 222)

While Sandra Elliot uses this example to focus on the researcher/screener, I want to use it to illustrate that the respondents or potential 'patients' are not blank slates. Women are steeped in knowledge of PND gleaned from the media, from experts they encounter face to face while having and caring for babies, from conversations with friends, post-natal support groups and from making their own sense of their experiences (see Chapters 4 to 6). Scientific validity is not a static phenomenon, nor can it ever be taken for granted that it is value-free, however stringent the controls that are imposed upon the research process or clinical trial.

Qualitative research, PND and science

'Qualitative research' is a generic term which refers to a range of approaches and methods to a scientific investigation (see Chapter 3). Qualitative research has been ignored by mainstream researchers and clinicians, first because it has been seen as 'biased', 'unscientific', 'ungeneralisable'. Second, it is seen as relatively expensive as the data are time-consuming to collect and analyse. Third, there have been few attempts to replicate qualitative studies; thus there is little evidence to demonstrate validity and reliability.

Qualitative research (if taken seriously) is not a retreat from rigour, however, but represents an intent to move towards the complex side of human experience and interaction – and, if used well, it provides a rigorous means of understanding what is often considered 'anecdote'. It is fundamentally different from traditional quantitative approaches to research, but this is its strength and the two approaches taken seriously are complementary – they do not have to clash. Although the results of a small-scale qualitative study may not be generalisable in the statistical sense, it is possible to identify common features and hypothesise that they may hold good for a population beyond the immediate sample.

Much has been written about qualitative research, over the last three or four years in particular, which has been helpful in clarifying epistemological issues, appropriate types of research question, the variety of qualitative methods, means of data analysis and how to prepare and present qualitative proposals and research findings (Munhall, 1994). Qualitative research is gaining an acceptable profile among health researchers, including academic clinicians. As Pope and Mays (1995), in an article in the traditionalist *British Medical Journal*, suggest:

> Qualitative studies are concerned with answering questions such as 'What is X and how does X vary in different circumstances, and why?' rather than 'How many Xs are there?'. Psychologists specifically ask 'What is it like to experience Y?' and 'How do people make sense of Z in the context of their own lives?'

It is important that scientific knowledge-claims about PND are challenged, informed and mediated by these kinds of questions, because they are complementary to the traditional questions and particularly because they provide direct evidence on women's experiences of PND and give these issues priority over the traditional means of deliberation as outlined in Chapters 2 and 3.

In contrast to the medical and social science models discussed there, PND, as described by the respondents in this research through the course of in-depth interviews, has a variety of meanings and the term is applied to a range of experiences. It is also clear that particular people – or the same people at various times – will label a depressing experience differently depending on their mood when they reflect upon it, their memory and the person they are addressing. All these issues are important for researchers and clinicians but tend to be ignored and trivialised for those in pursuit of publishable data.

Myth

Popular myths are subject to even less scrutiny than science. Myths pervade the knowledge of scientists, clinicians and lay people. In one account of therapy offered to depressed women after childbirth the authors suggest:

> A major concern of many postnatally depressed women is guilt at the burden their illness places on their spouses, even as they feel cut off from them and their family. Several mothers have told us that they found relief and comfort in knowing that, for once, therapy was directed to themselves as people, rather than them as mothers or members of a family.
>
> (Watson and Foreman, 1994: 233–4)

This paragraph is on the one hand clearly positive and ratifies women's distressing post-natal experiences. However, in dealing with women's role in the family in this way, this extract inadvertently reveals the misogyny, at least of the text if not the therapeutic intervention. Women, here, as in the majority of accounts of PND, are treated as the 'other' and viewed directly through male eyes. Do women feel guilty because they are depressed? Does the opportunity for therapy make someone feel 'comfort'? All 'sick' or injured people probably have guilt feelings if they are receiving high levels of care and especially if they themselves are being 'awkward' and unrewarding as patients, as many in that situation are perceived to be.

Data on psychological responses to being chronically sick, dying, and traumatic or disruptive life events more precisely demonstrate an intense *anger* rather than guilt. Findings from research in these cases make that anger explicit. Respondents of both sexes demand to know why this has happened to them (Kubler-Ross, 1970; Nicolson, 1994; 1995b). If women with PND are *sick*, why is there no expectation on the part of researchers that such women might experience anger, in common with other sick people? Why don't traditional researchers ask women about anger? The established PND literature fails to take account of anger as part of the 'syndrome'. Neither the Pitt measure of atypical depression following childbirth (Pitt, 1968), the Beck Depression Inventory (Huffman *et al.*, 1990) nor the EPDS (see Chapters 2 and 3) asks about anger. Issues about memory, irritability, being panicky, overwhelmed, unhappy, sleepless and even blaming 'myself unnecessarily when things went wrong' (Holden, 1994) are interrogated, but anger at being 'ill' in this way appears to be judged as irrelevant. Is this because 'women' don't get angry? Is the idea of anger too much at odds with mythical notions of femininity? Is it because women who are mothers are 'fulfilled' and PND is an explicable pathology while anger is not?

In my study, throughout all the women's accounts, there is an undercurrent of rage. They are angry with the midwives, doctors, hospital policies, the way they are treated, their own bodies, their behaviours, their circumstances, the losses they feel (see Chapter 6 and Nicolson, 1988). Far from feeling guilty and a burden to their partners, they express fury at the man for not being prepared to change while they themselves do the work and make the compromises. Boyd and Sellers (1982) conducted a survey on the 'British Way of Birth', commissioned for the TV programme *That's Life* hosted by Esther Rantzen, who claimed that she had experienced PND with the birth of her children and believed it was due to a hormone imbalance. They spend several pages quoting letters from women and some from men about their reactions to pregnancy, birth and the early post-natal weeks. Some made the point that men are equally responsible for the baby coming into the world and should not be 'left out'. They quote Derek:

> There is one point, however, we are disappointed about: the survey was only addressed to the mother, not to the father as well. It is a fact of life that it takes two people to produce a child, why exclude the father in the care of it?
>
> (Boyd and Sellers, 1982: 197)

His wife Silkie, apparently in support of his view and the way he conducted his role, says:

> It is a matter of our convenience that my husband goes out to earn the money and I look after household and child. But this does not mean that our baby would be as healthy as it is without the support of his father. If my husband did not care about our child, I would have had a rotten time during pregnancy, because he might not be willing to put up with my tiredness and bad moods. If he had not cared for our unborn child, he would not have supported me in suffering pains during pregnancy rather than taking painkillers which might have damaged the child (that meant a bad tempered wife for him). He might not give me a helping hand when I am worn out through breast feeding. He would just say, 'Put him on the bottle, then you will be less exhausted and more fun for me'. Surely the husband is a major factor in the well-being of the baby, a healthy pregnancy, a healthy birth and a healthy child.
>
> (Boyd and Sellers, 1982: 198)

The authors comment that they have included Silkie and Derek's comments in full in order to represent 'the feelings of those couples who approach childbirth in a spirit of equality' (Boyd and Sellers, 1982: 197). But where is the concern for the woman – the mother of the child – in this image? While no one has the right to claim to know exactly what Silkie means, there seems to be a subtext in which she portrays herself as an invisible martyr. Her use of terms such as 'suffering' pain and 'worn out' by breast-feeding being in both cases 'supported' by Derek emphasise his insensitivity to her torment. He is, it seems, encouraging her to continue with the very actions that are causing her distress.

Silkie's words here correspond in detail to the anger expressed by many of the women I interviewed (see Chapter 6). Data from the *That's Life* survey further endorse their accounts, particularly their experiences with the babies' fathers. Some women were positive about the fathers, although never without qualification. In these cases men were presented as potentially supportive but not really up to the role of full-time carer.

> For a man he's great. But I think no man can ever really understand just what a woman feels and experiences at this time.
>
> (p. 198)

> I couldn't have got through the birth without him and I can't imagine how I'll cope when he goes back to sea (although I will!).
>
> (p. 196)

The fathers do not allow the existence of a baby to make long-term changes to their lives. It is women whose lives have to change. It is the women, then, who have to manage not only the practical tasks surrounding baby and child-care (hard as they are); they have to manage the emotions that accompany such fundamental changes.

The baby's father is essential, of course, to the overall process of having a baby; but for a man to *father* in the sense of taking child-rearing as one of his day-to-day priorities might require him to renegotiate a sense of subjective masculinity. To be recognised as being *able* to father a child through inseminating a woman reinforces masculinity, but despite beliefs about the new man (see Chapter 6) this image upholds another myth. Disruption and the change of life style which caring for a baby demands lead to what Marris called a 'breakdown of interpretative structure' which may only be redeemed by the imposition of a new structure which brings with it new habits of thought (Marris, 1978: 133). For a man this would involve rethinking his sense of masculinity and what it is legitimate to do as a man, while for a woman it is seen to be the natural progression into fulfilled femininity – motherhood. Thus the day-to-day routine of child-care reinforces the differences between men's and women's lives and underpins the social construction of femininity and masculinity.

This is illustrated in my own work (Chapter 6) and that outlined in the *That's Life* survey (see pp. 198–9). Men are described there in much the same way as the women I interviewed described their babies' fathers:

> He does intend to be helpful and says things like 'Don't do the washing up, I'll do it' but two hours later it's still sitting there – so I do it and then he gets angry with me.

> … my husband thinks I'm grumbling about nothing.

... most men feel we can cope with all the extra work plus disturbed nights and also keeping the rest of the family happy, not realising how tired we get and offering that bit of extra help. Mine still likes his cup of tea in bed before getting up, so do I, but not a chance!

He feels that his job is from 8.30 a.m. to 5.00 p.m. and is very tiring – mine is apparently twenty-four hours a day and seven days a week. He doesn't feel obliged to help in the work of caring for the children.

The meaning of post-natal depression

Why are women seen as sick when they react to losses and isolation with depression when men, it seems, cannot even begin to cope with adapting to parenthood? Depression is a commonplace and rational reaction to the circumstances I have described. Many women continue to get depressed during the post-natal period.[1] Is this post-natal depression? Is there any value in such labelling?

It is clear that birth is painful and stressful, whatever the outcome. Women usually go into labour after nine months of excitement, worry, uncertainty about the baby; they are exhausted from carrying increased weight and generally, especially towards the end, keen to have the delivery behind them. Labour can be a frightening experience because of the uncertainty at each stage, and women ask themselves: how long will it last, how painful will it be, how well will I handle the pain, will the staff be competent and what will I think of the baby?

Lyons (1998) shows in her exploration of the clinical implications of post-traumatic stress (PTSD) following birth for first-time mothers, that there are a range of subjective and individual factors which impinge upon women's assessments of their deliveries and influence outcome. This is reiterated by Allen (1998), using qualitative methodology, specifically focusing upon traumatic labour. Both suggest that little is known yet about the long-term consequences of experiences of traumatic childbirth, not only for the mother herself, but for her perceptions of the child and of herself as a parent.

Mandy and colleagues (1998) challenge the view that childbirth and the post-partum directly precipitate PND. By demonstrating the prevalence of depressive symptoms across three groups – women having babies, women having non-gynaecological surgery and a control group of students reporting stress – they argue that it remains highly legitimate to continue to question the specific link between the physiology of the post-partum and subsequent depression.

Green (1998) argues provocatively that PND is not necessarily post-natal and not necessarily depression. PND has come to be seen as a quick and easy label

---

1   The post-natal period usually refers to the twelve months immediately following birth, although increasingly there is support for the view that depression may continue until the child starts school (see Brown and Harris, 1978; Chapter 2 in this volume).

to apply to a woman with appropriate symptoms who has had a baby. However, Green asserts that the Edinburgh Postnatal Depression Scale (EPDS) widely used as a screening instrument actually measures low mood or general dysphoria rather than clinical depression. She further challenges the notion that it is the physiology of childbirth and the post-partum that precipitates depression, citing the abundant evidence of depression in pregnant women which continues after the birth.

When I was working on my thesis I rejected the term 'PND' because it implied that women's experience of depression at this stage of their lives was pathological and intrinsically linked to female biology (Nicolson, 1988). I argued, for these reasons and because of the diversity of my findings about women's experience, that PND does not exist because depression following childbirth is a rational, predictable and healthy response to loss (Chapter 6). However, taking this position risks further marginalising the evidence of women's experience of the transition to motherhood and associated emotional responses. Recognition of this risk led me to use the term 'PND' to describe the focus of this work. This does not mean that my research and traditional approaches to the subject are entirely compatible: both are trying to make their own kind of sense of the same sets of behaviours and experiences.

However, the acceptance and use of labels such as PND implies a common understanding of PND as an entity. There is a shared belief that the same 'thing' is being observed, measured and treated whenever the label is applied.

The existence since the late 1980s of a developing critique demonstrating the way the medical profession in particular has pathologised the female body does make it possible to use the *term* while criticising the mechanisms by which it is understood (see also Barclay and Lloyd, 1996). It is easier to challenge researchers and clinicians within the terminology of the common language and so I have chosen to accept the term 'PND' as being as valid for the points that *I* make about women's lives as mothers as it is for patriarchal scientists.

Almost without exception women get depressed to some extent when they become mothers but the reasons for this are more complex by far than the traditional research has the power to identify. Those who do not get noticeably depressed feel the need to explain why they do not. Those who do get depressed find it easy to explain why they are (see Chapters 5 and 6). This is no surprise. Accounts of what it is like to be a mother in the early weeks, months or even years show pain and suffering as well as pleasure. And yet mainstream researchers and clinicians are still looking for the answer to this 'illness'. The view that adaptation to motherhood for any woman is easy remains widely held. Scientists and clinicians maintain the idea that depression is pathological – they want to screen for it and act in a preventive capacity. It is in their interests to focus on the reaction as an illness rather than recognise the diversity of responses or the tenacity and resilience of most women who experience depression as part of their individualised strategy of coping with stress, loss and change.

Post-natal depression needs to be reconceptualised as part of the *normal experi-*

ence of most women when they become mothers. This is not the same as saying that women need to be aware that their hormones are raging after birth, to imply that mothers are irrational, or that extraneous and dislocated sets of feelings will develop. Women and men have to understand the consequences of motherhood in the context of western industrial life in the absence of kinship networks, in the face of financial struggle, gender inequalities and gender power relations in the family.

Conclusions

Despite variations in reports and experiences, the data derived from my study provide some evidence to link experiences of depression in childbirth and early mothering. They are not common features of a 'syndrome' or illness, however, but associated with the shared problems surrounding the conditions of motherhood and thus expectations about the character of *women's* lives. Motherhood is tough, but so is life. No one woman's experience of mothering can be matched with another's or with another of her own experiences, because lives differ. However, human beings need space, time and support to adapt to loss and change. They need help when faced with added burdens, responsibility and social isolation. This is generally acceptable, it seems, in all cases but that of becoming a mother. Depression is considered a healthy part of the process of reintegration following loss most of the time, so why is it not conceptualised in a similar way for the losses following childbirth and motherhood? The ultimate myth that motherhood is natural and desirable means that women take on its burden unconditionally.

Psychology as an academic discipline ignores women's lives and fails to take gender seriously as a focus for analysing human behaviour beyond a crude variable to identify sex differences. Even so, psychology has much to say about women, what they should be like and particularly where they fail. Women's lives are described, controlled and constrained according to patriarchal precedents within a framework of patriarchal knowledge. Women are the 'other', their bodies and minds are 'deficient' in relation to the 'norm', which is set by the behaviour and attitudes of men. Men see women as mothers, and thus it is problematic if women do not adapt without qualms to motherhood. If women cannot mother, then who will care for infants and children? If women do not want to do it, or question whether the role should fall naturally to them because of their sex, then the consequences for men are alarming.

Men, at present, seem psychologically unimpaired by the experience of becoming a father, because they do it for status and pleasure (Lewis, 1986). Scientists do not ask questions about men's post-natal reactions alongside those they ask of women. If they did, then the extent of women's responsibilities would be exposed, making it difficult to pin the label 'illness' on PND. Reconsideration of women's descriptions of the fathers' behaviours makes this point. Is it normal to turn to alcohol because a baby's crying prevents sleep (as with Isobel's husband)? Is it normal for someone to carry on as they did before the birth with their working and social life (see Chapter 6)? Is it normal *not* to become emotionally involved in the life of the infant you have just fathered? Is it not potentially dangerous for a parent to take extended periods away from the infant during the first few post-natal months? We do not have the answers to these questions *because scientists have not asked them*. Why not? It is assumed that women will take child-care responsibility, that they will know what to do in the infant's best interests and will continue to provide domestic support for the father. But it is not just women who choose to have children. It is not just women who have an emotional and material invest-ment in producing a family. The family, science, knowledge and myth are all products of the society in which the family exists. We all have a responsibility to understand what underpins our knowledge of taken-for-granted assumptions. It is time that psychologists asked different kinds of questions about women's moth-ering and the role of the scientific method in understanding and explaining PND.

APPENDIX I

Profiles of the participants

Introduction

The information about recruitment of respondents is detailed in Appendix II. Profiles and reproductive histories are presented briefly below, based on information obtained during the interviews which took place between 1986 and 1987. I hope that these brief profiles will provide a little background to the respondents and contextualise the extracts quoted throughout the book. For full case studies see Nicolson, 1988. Details of their living arrangements, social class and birth histories are summarised in the following tables. All names have been changed.

Jane Johnson

Jane, originally from south London, had lived with Robert, her boyfriend, for four years. He was from the Middle East, and even though they were not legally married they had a Muslim wedding to please his family. They lived in a two-bedroomed flat in London's docklands.

I first met her only three weeks before their daughter's birth. She was very smartly dressed, shy but articulate. She reported that she did not feel happy in the mornings until she had her make-up on and her hair done. She was anxious about impending motherhood, but only admitted this on the third interview. She has always seen herself as 'feminine', wanting to look pretty, and although she wanted and expected to have children she lacked confidence that she would be good at baby-care.

Jane demonstrated a mixed picture of frustration and loneliness which was kept at bay by her satisfaction with the baby and support from her mother. Her partner was apparently ambivalent in his support and some of the positive things she said about him did not always coincide with her descriptions of his behaviour.

Lynn Ashton

Lynn had been married to Jonathan for nine years and they lived in a terraced house in a working-class part of London although she herself was from a middle-class family in the north of England. Her family were involved in politics, as she

Table A1 Pregnancy, reproductive and social information

Name	Number of interviews	Weeks pregnant at first interview	Number of previous children	Terminations and miscarriages	Type of delivery
Jane	4	35	0	0	normal
Lynn	4	33	0	0	normal[1]
Isobel	4	35	0	0	normal
Gwen	3	30	0	1[2]	normal
Frances	3[3]	35	1	0	normal
Dion	1	36	1	0	–
Matilda	3[3]	35	0	0	Caesarean
Samantha	3[3]	35	0	0	normal
Shirley	4	25	0	2[2]	planned induction
Meg	3	33	2	0	normal
Adrienne	2	22	1	1[4]	normal
Sylvia	4	32	0	0	normal
Sharon	4	29	0	0	normal
Penelope	4	32	0	0	premature
Sarah	3[3]	28	0	0	normal
Natasha	4	36	0	1[2]	Caesarean
Angela	4	36	1	0	normal
Hilary	3	24	1	0	normal
Jerri	4	31	0	0	Caesarean
Ruth	3[3]	19	0	1[2]	normal
Melanie	4	31	0	2[4]	normal
Norma	4	36	0	0	normal[1]
Wendy	3[3]	16	0	0	normal
Felicity	4	22	0	0	normal

Notes
1 Delivery took place in hospital although a home delivery had been planned
2 Termination
3 Three interviews plus a completed and returned questionnaire
4 Miscarriage

was herself. She described herself as 'determined', and whatever she does (including pregnancy) she throws herself into, with strong views on how it should be done. She was keen to include the baby in her life rather than build a different life around it.

She had hoped to become a mother earlier in her life, and had been trying to get pregnant for the previous seven years. She had found pregnancy 'wonderful' and had come to love the independent midwife she had arranged to care for her and to supervise a home delivery.

However, she had had to go into hospital to have the baby because after eighteen hours the midwife considered that she ought to have an epidural and speed up the contractions. She found over the following months that she needed (and received) much support from her husband and other family members.

Table A2 Occupational and marital status

Name	Age	Marital status	Occupation prior to pregnancy	Occupation after the baby	Partner's occupation
Jane	21	single	telephonist	none	machinist
Lynn	31	married	local politics	consultancy	optician
Isobel	30	married	dietician	dietician	teacher
Gwen	27	married	secretary	none	contracts manager
Frances	35	married	publisher	publisher	solicitor
Dion	23	single	shop assistant	not known	driver
Matilda	26	married	student	student	student
Samantha	27	married	computer supervisor	computer supervisor	postman
Shirley	35	single	press officer	press officer	antiques dealer
Meg	33	married	none	none	bank manager
Adrienne	30	married	none	none	barrister
Sylvia	29	married	antique dealer	none	solicitor
Sharon	33	married	none	none	businessman
Penelope	41	single	lecturer	lecturer	surveyor
Sarah	32	married	social worker	social worker	social work manager
Natasha	23	single	payroll supervisor	none	printer
Angela	32	married	none	none	lorry driver
Hilary	34	married	housing officer	housing officer	academic
Jerri	29	single	none	none	plumber
Ruth	31	married	lecturer	none	industrial manager
Melanie	35	married	civil servant	civil servant	lorry driver
Norma	27	married	midwife	midwife	hospital technician
Wendy	32	married	caterer/trainer	caterer/trainer	council worker
Felicity	31	married	scientist	scientist	economist

Isobel Williamson

Isobel had been married to Graham for four years. She had left Scotland at that time to live with him in a small flat in south London. This meant she was isolated from her roots and family. However, she saw herself as an independent person who 'doesn't need to be running in and out of other people's houses'.

Isobel was formal and neat in appearance, with short brown hair. She punctuated most of what she said with nervous laughter. She said that she wanted to take part in this study because she 'approved of research'. She was ambivalent about her career and wanted to have another baby fairly soon after this one. This pregnancy had been part of the couple's 'long-term plans'.

However, she found Rowan's arrival a great shock, and although Graham was very supportive at first, he himself got very stressed and anxious about fatherhood, particularly when he couldn't stop the baby crying and didn't get enough sleep. By the time he was six months, however, Rowan cried less relentlessly and Isobel was looking forward to returning to work. They did, however, plan to leave London as soon as Graham could find a suitable teaching post.

The main change she felt in herself was that she had lost her figure and was not 'young' any more. She said she was neither elated nor depressed: 'Just keeping my head above water. Just managing to cope with every day … but I feel I've got to put effort into getting that far.'

Gwen Abbot

Gwen lived in south-west London with Stan, her husband of four years, who was ten years older than she was. She was well groomed, with highlighted blond hair and immaculate nails and make-up. She was assertively 'non-ambitious' in her secretarial career, although she was dismissive of silly, stay-at-home women who corresponded with her image of her own mother. She wanted to confine her ambitions to family life and having a bigger and better home over the course of time. Her interests were gardening and attending to her dogs.

Gwen was concerned with her body image and had had previous episodes of putting on and losing weight in a dramatic way. The weight gain had been accompanied by depression. Thus she was particularly concerned about her pregnant body and relieved that her husband, a rugby player who was supportive of her keeping slim and fit, did not mind too much. The pregnancy had been a shock to them both, but they were reconciled in a positive way to starting a family.

Gwen herself had been born at home and, after some effort persuading various GPs in the area, managed to arrange a home delivery. However, when Hazel was born, she had a long and difficult labour, and was briefly admitted to hospital for an epidural and forceps delivery.

At the time of the third interview she tried to stop my coming by saying she didn't have post-natal depression, although agreed in the end to tell me about her experiences anyway. She was clearly very tense and angry that Stan was not as good and supportive as a father as she had hoped and expected. She did, however, want to have another child as soon as she could because: 'When all the pieces have knitted back together you can start your life again rather than have a gap. And then I think "Oh I don't have to go through all that again, do I?" '.

Frances Blake

Frances had been married to Philip for eleven years. They already had a 5-year-old son, Roland, and lived in a London suburb. Frances was well dressed and made-up, with a pleasant manner. She was always welcoming but as each interview progressed appeared increasingly 'distracted'. Listening to the tapes, I found that I was frequently 'prompting' her while she was pausing. Although I warmed to her, there didn't seem to be much rapport, although in several ways she was prepared to be revealing about emotional issues.

She had the second child for the sake of her son and did not want any more than two children. Initially she had seen how friends had been tied down with their children, but on becoming a mother herself she had few regrets.

She employed a nanny after Wendy was born. She was breast-feeding, and although she did not like being 'cow-like' and had some difficulties, she persisted because she believed it important. Her mother and husband had been supportive over the early days so 'I got through my so called post-natal depression time without being depressed'. The feeding caused the greatest distress, and although Wendy was a good baby, Roland had difficulties with the idea of a new sister, which worried Frances.

She found herself getting tired and with some bad moments of depression even when Wendy was six months. She did not consider herself a particularly good mother, which dented her confidence. 'I feel depressed at my apparent inadequacy.'

Dion Scotland

Dion, a black woman born in south London, had her roots in the West Indies. However, she had several relatives including her parents living nearby. She lived with the father of her second child in a council flat in a dreary tower block, although the inside of the flat was cheerful and comfortable. She worked in a supermarket in the evenings and therefore shared child-care with her boyfriend. She didn't seem to enjoy being interviewed and continued to put her hair in rollers throughout the time I was there.

She said she did not believe her boyfriend would make a good or reliable father, particularly in relation to money, although she was really happy to be pregnant again. She was dreading the birth. 'I'm more scared than someone who's not been through it.' She was very keen to get herself back into a slim shape again afterwards.

Matilda Biamma

Matilda's baby was due three weeks before she entered the third year of a four-year undergraduate course in sociology. She had been married to Desmond for eighteen months, but at the time he was studying for a Ph.D. in Africa. Matilda herself came, as a teenager, from Zimbabwe as a refugee. She had had a difficult time on arriving in England, expecting white British people to be liberals, but in fact experiencing racism and isolation, especially when she had been working in Yorkshire as a nurse. She was happier being a student in London.

Two things had always been important to her – becoming a mother and becoming a professional person. She never considered choosing between career and motherhood. Thus she had looked forward to her pregnancy and becoming a mother. Matilda's pregnancy was difficult, particularly because she had to go through most of it without the support of her husband.

After the baby was born she moved from student residences to stay with an aunt in another part of London. Her husband had not come over in time for the birth and so she handled it alone. It had been very difficult. She had been in intense pain and eventually was rushed to the operating theatre as the baby's heartbeat became weaker.

When the baby was about three months old she was taken back to Africa by Matilda's mother so that Matilda could finish her course. Although this was traditional in her culture, and planned in advance (it did, however, surprise *me* at the time), she had mixed feelings about it. 'I keep thinking "I must be wicked to do that to my own baby" '. Ansiet, her daughter, was always on her mind and she felt that being a mother had changed her and made her stronger despite the fact that she did not have her baby with her.

'My husband, friends and family seem to appreciate me more. I actually have had more energy and more determination to get on with my career.'

Samantha Foster

Samantha was twenty-seven and had been married to Eric, a postman, for six years. She was a supervisor in a word-processing company and had developed a career from being an unambitious office worker. She came from a large family which had not been all that happy, partly because of poverty and a sense of being 'overcrowded' and no one had cared about education or career. Her abilities and success had isolated her from her former friends and relatives. She was constantly worried about her weight.

She was the first generation of her family to live in owner-occupied accommodation and she and Eric had renovated a flat and then moved to the house they lived in at the time of the pregnancy. She is clear that she wants her children to have a better start in life than she felt she had had. She had never been close to her mother and had hardly spoken to her father until she was in her teens and found her parents to be always stressed and tired. Her relationship with her husband had been the only satisfactory one she had ever had.

She did not like Ellie when she first saw her, partly because of marks left by forceps used during delivery. She found she resented having to care for her immediately following a tiring labour. 'I thought I'd have at least one night to catch up on my sleep!'. She also had trouble with breast-feeding, which she found stressful.

Gradually, though, she managed to cope with the baby and loved her very early on. Eric was very supportive and returned home in the early afternoon to take over either housework or child-care.

By three months after delivery she had lost weight and was feeling much happier. She was also feeling more confident about returning to her office. She had attended the firm's Christmas party and was delighted to report that she had been treated like an adult person rather than a 'mother'. Although she enjoys motherhood, she would not be happy only to be at home. She adapted successfully to her return to work and although when she finished breast-feeding felt that some closeness between herself and Ellie had gone, the experience of parenthood had brought her closer to Eric.

Shirley Hampson

Shirley was thirty-five years old and lived with Mike, a self-employed antiques dealer who was going to be mainly responsible for child-care once Shirley returned to work as a press officer for a trade union.

Shirley did not like to talk about her feelings. She had decided to have a baby because she felt time had been running out, but had found the decision difficult. Her sister had had a baby the previous year and so she thought that it would be good for cousins to be of similar ages, which is what eventually decided her on the timing of the event. She had worked out the details of the division of labour between herself and Mike.

Her ambition was eventually to have a successful political career but she did not have any clear idea of what she would be like as a mother as she had not given the details of motherhood much thought.

Anna was born after an eight-hour planned induction. She found herself at ease with the baby but very tired and, although Mike would take over baby-care sometimes, she considered that she took the lion's share of the work. Shirley was planning to return to work full-time and had arranged a nanny share. She felt she did not want any more children because 'I'm not prepared to make the sacrifices you need to make if you have more than one'.

Meg Davidson

Meg, thirty-three years of age, had trained and worked as a maths teacher until she had her first child. Brian, her husband, was a bank manager and they had three children between them. She had become pregnant by accident and was shocked because she 'didn't want to go through it all again. I'd spent eight years being a mum and wanted to do something else.' She had just returned to teaching.

She had felt very tired throughout the pregnancy and in fact had become seriously ill following the delivery of William.

She had recovered, though, by the time William was six months and had considered getting a supply teaching post. She sometimes felt quite depressed and coped with it by trying to get some rest. She had joined the parent–teacher association at her older children's school 'so I could get out of the house and meet new people' and was also considering doing an Open University course.

Adrienne Winters

Adrienne, married to Philip for eight years, was thirty. She worked as a freelance cook (doing dinner parties and lunches in people's homes) and Philip was a barrister. She came from a rich family and her unearned income enabled Philip to leave his previous job and study for the bar. They lived in a large detached house in a private road near a Royal Park and all their healthcare and proposed education was to be private.

The couple already had a young son, Bobby, for whom she employed a nanny and she had another nanny and maternity nurse arranged for when the second child was born. Her second child was another boy and because she had particularly wanted to have a girl she was already planning a third child.

She thought that having two children was very difficult and she especially had problems with the nanny and maternity nurse being 'too demanding'.

She was a friend of Sylvia's, but was dismissive of her, describing her and her husband as '*Guardian* readers'. Adrienne was particularly scathing about Sylvia's husband because he bathed the baby. She did not like to see men so involved in child-care.

Adrienne had had problems with her first delivery and had been ill for some months afterwards. She was clear that no one needs to be depressed.

Sylvia Morgan

Sylvia, an antiques dealer, was twenty-nine. She was married to Mark, a solicitor who had been a close friend for some time before they started seeing each other as a couple.

They decided to have a baby because several of their friends were doing so and it therefore seemed to be the right time.

Sylvia, who had an old back injury, had an unpleasant experience of delivery because no one on duty at the time would pay attention to her pleas to choose her own birth position even though she had been assured that her case was well documented in the medical notes.

She gave birth to a daughter, Felicity, for whom she employed a maternity nurse. However, she found the nurse more of a problem than she found coping with things herself and eventually dismissed her.

She did become stressed and 'fraught' at times over the first six months and found her husband less supportive than she thought he would be. However, overall she considered that motherhood suited her but she did want to return to work and keep something of herself intact.

Sharon Wilson

Sharon was thirty and had been married to Barry for seven years. They had delayed having children because they enjoyed their social life too much, but in the end they felt they had to 'take the plunge'. Sharon came from a rich farming family originally and had worked as a secretary after leaving school. Barry was a businessman with a large salary but during the time I was interviewing Sharon his company was taken over and his job was at risk.

She wanted to see herself as 'unconventional' and was determined to avoid talking about nappies and babies as she saw many of her friends doing.

She desperately wanted and had a boy. She became very attached to him and felt content being at home, certainly over the first two months. However, her husband kept trying to persuade her to leave the baby with a babysitter and continue their social life, which she was not particularly happy about. So that Barry 'doesn't get bored in the evening, we have friends in for drinks, but it is still difficult to put off going out'.

She found herself getting very cross and frustrated with Barry in ways that had never been the case before, although by the time the baby was six months old she found herself getting back to normal. However, 'I think I vary enormously. I swing backwards and forwards. One minute I'm really optimistic and the other I'm down about things.'

When she received a letter from the 'temp' agency she used to work for asking whether she was available for work she felt it gave her a 'buzz' that she had been useful in the world out there. However, she intended to have another baby as soon as she could and did not want to work when the children were young so she refused.

Penelope Holt

Penelope was forty-one, the oldest first-time mother in the study. She was living 'part-time' with Roger, who had only half left his wife, and two teenage children. She was a college lecturer and he was a local government officer. He had mixed feelings about being a father again but Penelope had been clear that she had wanted the pregnancy to continue as it might be her only chance to have a baby as she had believed herself infertile.

She had a difficult pregnancy and delivery, which she had to cope with on her own because Roger was on a camping holiday with his older children and could not be contacted.

Both she and Leah, her baby, were in hospital for several weeks. When Roger did arrive back from holiday, he was totally unsupportive and very stressed and anxious. He started to drink, get angry about being woken in the night and in fact left her several times for long periods. In the end he returned and decided to live full-time with Penelope. Although she accepted this, she felt that he had been so dreadful that she would never fully be able to forgive him. The whole experience of early motherhood 'had just overwhelmed me and I felt I was totally submerged by it'. However, she thinks the experience has overall made her stronger and that she could cope with anything in the future.

Sarah Beresford

Sarah, aged thirty-two, had been married to Norman for six years, and they lived in a west London suburb. They were both social workers although Norman was in a senior management post. Sarah was an ex-flatmate of Felicity's. Both Sarah and Norman come from middle-class families in the home counties.

The couple had been thinking for several years about having a baby but until Sarah was thirty they did not feel any urgency. She had a part-time post lined up for after her maternity leave and although she did feel ambivalent about returning after the birth, she was relieved when she did. Her own mother had devoted her whole life to child-care and mothering and she did not want that for herself, although she did want to be a good mother. Becoming a mother has changed her ('It's made me feel much more adult') and she believes she worries less about trivia. She did feel that she was always having to take care not to get too stressed and exhausted as that would make her depressed.

Natasha Barr

Natasha lived in Croydon with Josh, her fiancé. She gave up her job as a payroll supervisor when she found she was pregnant, but was a trained hairdresser and intended to work intermittently working in people's homes on a self-employed basis. Natasha was diabetic and so was booked into the large teaching hospital rather than the local one like the others from her antenatal group. She had an unhappy childhood which I agreed not to write about in any detail, and was not in regular contact with her family although Josh had several local relatives. She herself had local friends.

She had not been very pleased to be pregnant because she was unhappy to be so fat, as her appearance was very important to her. She wore jeans or a track suit at home but made the point that she would never wear such clothes outside the home and never when she was with Josh.

She liked to be organised around the house and had come to terms with the fact that Josh would do very little. This proved to be the case with child-care as well as housework. She considered that she was constantly stuck with the baby without support and although she would not have been without her she wanted to have a chance to have a break. 'I'm not depressed – I'm just pissed off.'

Angela Hilton

Angela, thirty-two, had been married to Mark, a long-distance, overnight lorry driver for five years and they already had a son, Jeremy, whom she described as a 'handful'. They lived in a small, three-bedroomed terraced house. She had previously been in the police as a member of the vice squad, which she had found exciting and compelling and although she had left that work some time previously, it still formed an important part of her identity. It had been her way of life rather than a job.

She had been what she had described as her 'daddy's girl', which influenced the way she thought about her social and familial role, and appreciated the fact that Mark worked at night and was able to take a reasonable share of child-care and domestic tasks.

She found her first son difficult to handle and also really suffered emotionally because she had become overweight. Also they were financially pressed.

She always attributed any feelings of depression to specific worries such as money, while Mark told her that she 'became depressed at the drop of a hat'. She worried about the children and also about the fact that she had lost control during the birth of her first child. This made her anxious about the second birth, of her son Carey, which in the event she handled well and felt overall better organised. However, she did become anxious and overwhelmed with depressed feelings on several occasions although she could only admit them to herself at the last interview, looking back. She found it very helpful to have the chance to talk to me about her feelings.

She found routine a problem and worried about her loss of independence, which she dated to not having a job rather than motherhood. She became particularly distressed when she found herself not getting interviewed for work that she would have considered beneath her previously.

Hilary Matthews

Hilary, thirty-four, with an 18-month-old daughter, was married to Ken, a lecturer. They had known each other for many years but only been married for four. Hilary was a senior local government officer and planned maternity leave as she had done with the first baby.

She felt she had bullied Ken into starting a family because he could never be decisive, but he was pleased once the baby arrived. She had been depressed and anxious the first time, feeling things were a bit out of her control. However, she felt more confident about child-care the second time. She felt acutely that the world of the 'mother' was different from the world of work and that mothers were treated as second-class, rather stupid citizens and she resented this.

The delivery was terrible in that she desperately wanted to avoid a Caesarean, which she had had the first time, but her body was literally ripped apart and the problems she had while she was healing did not ease her state of mind. However, she was proud that she had managed a normal delivery.

She did get stressed and anxious with the two young children and, although Ken clearly helped, she was not getting the degree of support she felt she needed.

Jerri Scott

Jerri, twenty-nine years old and expecting her first baby, was living with her fiancé Tom in south London. He was a self-employed plumber and Jerri did the accounts.

She had never felt maternal in any way although always expected she would have children. Her labour had been traumatic for her in that she had to have an emergency Caesarean and because they were not married a midwife created a fuss to try and prevent Tom from being present at the delivery. This was very stressful. It was also a very painful delivery and she had nightmares and flashbacks about it.

She worried about the baby's health although in fact there were no problems. By three months after the birth, Jerri started to believe that things were going well and by six months she and Tom had begun to think about having a second child and moving to the country. She felt that, despite ups and downs, most of the changes in her life brought about by motherhood were positive. Motherhood had made her into a more caring person who was not so much into 'image' as she had been beforehand.

Ruth Erikson

Ruth, thirty-one, chose to leave her job as a health visitor tutor when she became pregnant, although she eventually returned to work nearer home as a part-time health visitor. She had been married to Roy, a scientist, for two years although they had lived together previously.

Ruth's mother had killed herself, apparently due to post-natal disturbance, and this was at the forefront of her mind during her pregnancy and the early days of motherhood. She herself had been depressed and had threatened to overdose when she was in her late teens.

She had arranged to have the baby in hospital but on the 'domino' system through which she was discharged almost immediately under midwife care at home. Her stepmother was very supportive and stayed with them after the baby was born.

Ruth developed inflammation of her breasts shortly after her daughter's birth and did suffer some embarrassing panic attacks on the first few occasions she had to go out alone, for example in a supermarket when she realised she had forgotten her cheque book. Overall, she felt she survived the experience without any episodes of severe depression although she did worry about child-care a great deal.

Melanie Griffiths

Melanie, a high-ranking civil servant, was thirty-five when she had her baby and had been living with John, a long-distance lorry driver, albeit a graduate, whom she married two years prior to the interview. They agreed in advance that John would be the prime child-carer. When Charlotte was born Melanie took maternity leave, and chose to bottle-feed so that both she and John could take equal shares in night feeds. This meant that she was protected from some of the extremes of tiredness that she might have felt otherwise. She did have fears that John would gain all of Charlotte's attention but the compensation was that she had no doubts or fears about child-care, and thus was able to concentrate on her career. She considered that she gradually became far more ambitious during the post-natal months and her early return to work than she felt before having a baby. She attributed this to the increased responsibility and felt positively about this change.

Despite John's being at home, she considered that she had to organise the housework, shopping and cooking although overall she believed John made a better primary carer than she would have done.

Norma Brookes

Norma and Eli had been together three years, although married a few months prior to the interview because of the baby. She was a midwife and he was a hospital technician. Norma was from a large, middle-class Irish family and Eli from South America. Norma had been depressed in the past as a student nurse and was worried that she would get depressed post-natally. She was also worried about becoming the kind of mother she dreaded, who had no fun, was serious and unappealing. She had also been accepted to train as a health visitor before the pregnancy and so felt a bit upset that she would have to give that up and return to midwifery, at least for a while, because they needed money.

A home delivery was planned, but this did not happen because after several hours in labour Norma decided that she wanted to have the birth speeded up and was admitted to hospital. However, she felt guilty in the end that she had made that decision.

She became very possessive and anxious about her son, and she and Eli had many arguments and she felt her marriage was not what she had hoped. However, by six months after the birth she felt things had become more settled between them and she had managed to arrange child-care and return to work. However, she felt that she had changed dramatically, having become more serious and responsible than she had felt before the pregnancy.

Wendy Bridges

Wendy and Dave had been married for four years and both worked for a local authority in inner London. Wendy, however, had a more senior post, which seemed to be the source of some contention between them. Dave had a problem with alcohol and the couple had been on the verge of divorce but decided to try and have a baby in order to put things right.

Dave did not prove to be very supportive and Wendy found herself cooking for him and his brother shortly after leaving hospital and was bitterly resentful. However, she felt that Dave did enjoy the baby.

Wendy returned to work when Molly was three months old and believed that she had benefited psychologically a great deal from becoming a mother because it gave her an added dimension to life and enabled her to decide what things in life were the most important. Dave, she believed, did not put Molly first, in the way she thought he should, but he was a good father. Wendy considered that her relationship with Dave was on the whole unimproved by parenthood.

Felicity Pickett

Felicity was thirty-one and a scientist, married to Rob, with whom she had been living for around six years. They had decided not to have children because he had a grown-up family from his first marriage. However, as she became older, Felicity realised that she wanted at least one child of her own and Rob agreed.

She found her work stimulating but very hard and wanted to work part-time following her maternity leave and she worried about how she would manage her work and her baby a great deal. Part of her worry was that being a scientist was 'fundamental' to the person she considered herself to be. She also found that she worked closely and effectively with men and the experience of being in totally female company made her anxious. Her son Nick was born early and over the Christmas holiday, which meant both a shock and disruption to the family plans which she found disorienting. She was worried that it took her a few days to 'bond' with the baby, which she attributed to the early birth.

In the first few weeks she found organising her life was a 'monumental' task and felt that her sense of identity had been disrupted. Gradually, as she became more used to him and attended some work-related meetings, she felt less stressed and eventually she became bored with being at home as a full-time mother/housewife.

APPENDIX II
Methods

In order to set the data in context, I present the methodology in some detail. This is first to make clear that the evidence underlying the main arguments is not anecdotal but collected in a rigorous manner. Second, as with all science, detailed methodological issues make replication possible.

Sampling

Rationale

The design developed here, and discussed in Chapter 3, did not require systematic sampling in the traditional sense. I did not intend to make generalisations or predictions from the data. The major requirement was that the women recruited were willing to make a commitment of around ten hours of time. I also wanted the respondents to have enough verbal and intellectual competence to engage discursively with the topic of the transition to motherhood and emotional change. Thus my selection criteria were that the woman was pregnant, and that within the sample there was a reasonably broad range of age, class, race, parity, source and type of maternity care services planned. As only one researcher with limited time was involved, I further needed a manageable span of delivery dates.

Thus I interviewed women due to deliver babies between 1 August 1986 and the end of February 1987. The majority of births took place between September and November 1986.

Recruiting the sample

1   I contacted two pregnant students in the polytechnic where I worked. Both agreed to be interviewed, although one decided to move away from London to her parents' home and so I did not interview her (Matilda, Other).
2   I contacted a South London National Childbirth Trust teacher who referred one woman (Sharon).
3   A health visitor from east London referred one woman (Jane).
4   A health visitor tutor referred an acquaintance (Ruth).
5   The same tutor put me in touch with an ex-student of hers, by then a health

visitor in Croydon, who referred seven women from her mothercraft class (Natasha, Angela, Dion, Isobel, Samantha, Jerri, Meg).

6   There was a significant 'snowballing' effect.

    i   My cousin gave me the names of three pregnant friends (Shirley, Frances, Melanie). Melanie put me in touch with Felicity. Felicity told me of three pregnant friends (Sarah, Wendy, Other). All wanted to be interviewed but one lived in Brighton, which was a long way for me to travel.

    ii   Shirley put me in contact with three of her friends. All agreed to be interviewed, although one had a baby before I managed to see her (Penelope, Lynn, Other).

    iii   Lynn introduced me to two people she knew from her National Childbirth Trust class (Norma, Gwen) and an MP friend who initially agreed to be interviewed but then felt the overall time commitment would be too much (Other).

    iv   Sharon introduced me to a neighbour (Sylvia) who in turn introduced me to two of her friends (Adrienne, Other), one of whom agreed to be interviewed.

7   Finally, a colleague's wife (whom I did not know) agreed to be interviewed (Hilary).

I contacted the women by letter, enclosing an acceptance form to ensure informed consent and SAE. If they returned this, I telephoned to arrange an interview and explain more about the research. Some women were contacted directly by phone (Gwen, Norma and the women from the mothercraft class in Croydon).

Twenty-nine pregnant women in total were approached. One refused outright, another withdrew due to work pressure, another left the area, a fourth went into labour early, and another lived too far away for me.

The sampling which occurred in stages 1–3 above was relatively slow and took place from May to July 1986. Then the others were recruited rapidly during August.

Composition of the sample

The sample comprised twenty-four women whose ages ranged from 21 to 41 years on first interview. The average was 30.3 years. For eighteen women it was their first baby, for five their second and for one her third.

The age range for those having babies for the first time was 21 to 41 years, average age 30. Two had had at least one miscarriage, three had had at least one termination. All had a permanent relationship with the baby's father at first interview. Two had been married previously. Five others had had a long-term live-in relationship prior to the relationship with the baby's father. Two women were black, one West Indian in origin and one from Zimbabwe. Another was Irish although a permanent resident of London. The rest were white British and lived either in Croydon or inner London (north and south) although not all were born in London themselves.

There are inevitable weaknesses in such an *ad hoc* method of sampling because it is not collected in a traditional manner that makes generalisation appropriate – that is, randomised, stratified or representative. This was not my purpose anyway, as other research on PND had been carried out with these kinds of samples. The strength of this form of recruitment lies in the enthusiasm and commitment of the participants. My intention here was to focus on depth and subjectivity and thus being pregnant and a commitment to the research process were the vital ingredients.

Despite its limitations, the group I did interview was not homogeneous. The interview data demonstrated both a variety and commonality of experiences.

Techniques

Having prescribed the parameters of the study and stating the research problems and aims, it is clearly important to select methodologies and techniques to match. Thus it seemed that a semi-structured interview would be the most appropriate technique. However, its form needed careful consideration.

Following Bott (1957) and Rapoport and Rapoport (1976), whose research was also seeking to understand how respondents justified and explained their own lives, I decided that an interview guide (Appendix III) was the most appropriate means of data collection.

An interview guide enabled me to make comparisons between women while leaving scope for subjective meaning and the experience of each individual to be expressed. The interview guide would also offer the scope to establish some kind of internal validity by enabling women to express and explore some of the contradictions they felt when talking about their experiences. Finally, it seemed that an interview guide would be the most appropriate means of establishing a rapport with the respondent.

Thus the guide and a brief biographical data sheet were used for the first interview, while the subsequent ones were structured around getting the respondents to reflect on the intervening periods.

The interview process

The intention had been to interview the twenty-four participants on four occasions (see Table A3 which shows the final pattern of attrition).

The reasons for the attrition varied. Dion, who dropped out after Interview 1, had, I think, misunderstood the project.[1] Those who dropped out after the third

---

1 She lived in an impoverished area of south London in a high-rise council flat and after the first interview realised that there was nothing much in it for her. Retrospectively, I think she hoped that I might have been offering help with child-care and finance.

LIVERPOOL
JOHN MOORES UNIVERSITY
AVRIL ROBARTS LRC
TEL. 0151 231 4022

Table A3 Numbers of women interviewed at each stage

Interview 1 (pregnancy)	Interview 2 (1 month post-partum)	Interview 3 (3 months post-partum)	Interview 4 (6 months post-partum)
24 women	23 women	22 women	13 women

Total number of interviews = 82

interview did so for a number of reasons including returning to work. I only interviewed Meg three times because of the traumas of her delivery, during which she nearly died, so I combined Interviews 2 and 3 at two and a half months post delivery.

The women who did not have a fourth interview were sent a questionnaire when their baby was six months old. Only two failed to return this.

Interview 1

These initial interviews took place in the women's homes during the 16th and 35th weeks of pregnancy.[2] When I arrived I answered questions about what I was doing and why.[3] Then I showed them the interview guide so that they could have some idea of what I would be talking to them about, and also to give them an opportunity to refuse to talk about anything in advance, if they felt that way.

I then turned on the tape recorder and began by going through their biographical summary, which sometimes provided a stimulus for particularly relevant issues. If that seemed to be the case I pursued those themes (see Chapter 5), taking care to cover all the topics on the interview plan by the end of the interview. This flexibility enabled the respondent to stress the features of her life which had the most significance for her at the time. The interviewer's task was to keep to the specified parameters and follow up relevant areas via prompts such as: 'Could you say more about ...', 'How did that make you feel?' 'Why ...' and similar open-ended questions. When the researcher judged that discussion of a particular topic had been completed she would say: 'Is there anything else you consider to be important about "X"? and then: "Now could we move on to talk about "Y"?'

The tape was a 90-minute one, and I took a spare in case the interview time exceeded that. At the end of the interview I asked how they had felt about it. Most comments were positive. In addition to the tapes, I also made notes about my impressions immediately on leaving.

2 According to estimated times of delivery.
3 This was problematic in that I had to tell them I was interested in post-natal depression. However, I had decided in advance of recruitment that I would have to make this information public because I wanted to ask them about their own experiences of depression in the past.

Interview 2

The respondents were asked at Interview 2 to 'tell me about the baby's birth and what has happened/how you have felt since then'. By the second interviews the respondents had begun to make it clear they had 'saved up' what they wanted to say. (It had been suggested that they kept a diary as an *aide-mémoire*. This had clear implications for the process of reflexivity during the study (see Chapter 5).

The second interviews were on the whole briefer than the first, lasting between 35 and 90 minutes (50 minutes on average). The respondents were exhausted by the labour and the infant care, and most of the interviews were interrupted at points for changing nappies and feeding.

Interview 3

At Interviews 3 and 4 the respondents were asked to 'tell me what has happened/ how you felt since the last time we met'. The third interviews were longer (average 1 hour and 15 minutes). I asked them to report on progress and picked up on and pursued certain issues (see Chapter 5). Some women returned again to the birth and others focused on the future, which suggested that this period (three months after the birth) might be a turning point in the post-natal experience.

Interview 4

The fourth interview began very much as Interview 3 and was about the same length. The greatest differences emerged here in the topics that were discussed. Most women were back to being 'themselves' and identified their individual interests more specifically than in the middle two interviews.

Data

The tape recordings were transcribed verbatim. I did them all myself, and because I did not own a PC and was not a particularly fast typist, I transcribed them by hand.

The transcription in fact comprised the first stage of analysis because I outlined key passages and also made notes of my impressions of what was being said, some of which made an interesting comparison to the notes I had made immediately following the interview (see Chapter 5). There were several apparent contradictions, one frequently occurring when I felt certain interviews had been difficult but when the tapes did not give that impression and respondents were apparently talking more freely than they seemed to be face to face.

Analysis

Data analysis was carried out on up to four tapes (and in four cases, as explained above, the fourth interview was replaced by a written account) of between 50 and

90 minutes for each respondent. Each transcript was transcribed verbatim and examined for accounts of depression, including descriptions of moods/emotions which might be similar to this, and expressions of the relation between the woman's concepts of motherhood and the post-natal depression discourse.

APPENDIX III
Interview guide

INTERVIEW GUIDE: INTERVIEW 1

In this interview I would like to discuss the following with you:

I *Biography*

Name
Occupation/education of both you and the baby's father
Status of relationship with the baby's father
Number of previous children/step-children
Composition of household
Financial arrangements

II *Personal History*

Parents – status of their relationship, where, ages, occupation, relationship with you
Siblings – as above
Changes/movements of family in childhood and since
Schooling/achievements
Past and future occupational details/plans
Ambitions and aspirations/past and present
What led up to this pregnancy?

III *Relationships and Identity*

Reflections on childhood – friendships, siblings, parents
Influential people/events
Evaluation of self growing up: changes
Sexual experiences
Organisation of family life/expectations of changes
Expectations of parenthood: self/partner
Expectations of personal change

IV *Self and Disposition*

Experiences of depression/what was it like/how long/why
Expectations of depression re parenthood ideas about gender roles
Description of self: strengths and weaknesses
How much control do you want to have over your own life/expectations of changes after birth?

APPENDIX IV

Postal questionnaire
(sent six months after delivery)

Could you please write full answers to the first two questions below:[1]

1   Your baby is now 6 months old. Could you please describe any occasions you have felt 'down' or 'depressed' over that period (even if you have mentioned them to me before now)?

2   In what ways do you feel you have changed since I first interviewed you?

3   Could you please circle the answer that best describes how you feel at the present time:[2]

Do you sleep well?	Yes	No	Don't know
Do you easily lose your temper?	Yes	No	Don't know
Are you worried about your looks?	Yes	No	Don't know
Have you a good appetite?	Yes	No	Don't know
Are you as happy as you ought to be?	Yes	No	Don't know
Do you easily forget things?	Yes	No	Don't know
Do you have as much interest in sex as ever?	Yes	No	Don't know
Is everything a great effort?	Yes	No	Don't know
Do you feel ashamed for any reason?	Yes	No	Don't know
Can you feel the baby is really yours?	Yes	No	Don't know
Do you want someone with you all the time?	Yes	No	Don't know
Are you easily woken up?	Yes	No	Don't know
Do you feel calm most of the time?	Yes	No	Don't know
Do you feel you are in good health?	Yes	No	Don't know
Do you cry easily?	Yes	No	Don't know
Is your memory as good as it ever was?	Yes	No	Don't know
Have you less desire for sex than usual?	Yes	No	Don't know
Have you enough energy?	Yes	No	Don't know
Are you satisfied with the way you are coping with things?	Yes	No	Don't know
Do you worry a lot about the baby?	Yes	No	Don't know
Do you feel unlike your normal self?	Yes	No	Don't know
Do you have confidence in yourself?	Yes	No	Don't know

4   Is there anything else you would like to add about the way you feel at the moment?

---

1 Half a page of blank space followed each open-ended question.
2 This is the adapted Pitt measure of atypical depression following childbirth used in the pilot study (see Nicolson, 1986 and Chapter 3).

REFERENCES

Ainsworth, M.D. (1992) Attachments and other affectional bonds across the life cycle, in J. Stevenson-Hinde and P. Marris (Eds) *Attachment across the Life Cycle*, Routledge: New York

Alder, E. (1994) Sexuality after childbirth, in P.Y.L. Choi and P. Nicolson (Eds) *Female Sexuality: Psychology, Biology and Social Context*, Hemel Hempstead: Harvester

Allen, S. (1998) A qualitative analysis of the process, mediating variables and impact of traumatic childbirth, *Journal of Reproductive and Infant Psychology*, 16(1) (in press)

Anzlaone, M.K. (1977) Postpartum depression and premenstrual tensions; life stress and marital adjustment, Boston: Ph.D. thesis

Appleby, L. (1990) The aetiology of post partum psychosis: why are there no answers?, *Journal of Reproductive and Infant Psychology*, 8(2), 109–18

Apter, T. (1993) *Professional Progress: Why Women Still Don't Have Wives*, Basingstoke: Macmillan

Ashworth, P.D. (1979) *Social Interaction and Consciousness*, Chichester: Wiley

Badinter, E. (1981) *The Myth of Motherhood*, London: Souvenir Press

Ballinger, B., Buckley, D.E., Naylor, G.J. and Stansfield, D.A. (1979) Emotional disturbance following childbirth: clinical findings and urinary excretion of cyclic AMP, *Psychological Medicine*, 9, 293–300

Banister, P., Burman, E., Parker, I., Taylor, M. and Tindall, C. (1994) *Qualitative Methods in Psychology: A Research Guide*, Buckingham: Open University Press

Barclay, L.M. and Lloyd, B. (1996) The misery of motherhood: alternative approaches to maternal distress, *Midwifery*, 12, 136–9

Barzilai, S. and Davies, A.M. (1973) Postpartum mental disorders in Jerusalem: survey of hospitalised cases 1964–1967, *British Journal of Social Psychiatry and Community Health*, 6 (2), 80–9

Beckett, H. (1986) Cognitive developmental theory in the study of adolescent development, in S. Wilkinson (Ed.) *Feminist Social Psychology: Developing Theory and Practice*, Milton Keynes: Open University Press

Bem, S. (1993) *The Lenses of Gender*, New Haven: Yale University Press

Berger, P. (1966) Identity as a problem of knowledge, *Archives européennes de sociologie*, 7, 105–15

Berger, P. and Kellner, H. (1964/82) Marriage and the construction of reality, in M. Anderson (Ed.) *Sociology of the Family*, Harmondsworth: Penguin

Berger, P. and Luckmann, T. (1985) *The Social Construction of Reality*, Harmondsworth: Pelican

Bleier, R. (1984) *Science and Gender: A Critique of Biology and its Theories on Women*, Oxford: Pergamon Press

Blumfield, W. (1992) *Life after Birth: Every Woman's Guide to the First Year of Motherhood*, Shaftesbury, Dorset: Element

REFERENCES

Bott, E. (1957) *Family and Social Network*, London: Tavistock

Boulton, M.G. (1983) *On Being a Mother*, London: Tavistock

Bowlby, J. (1951) *Maternal Care and Mental Health*, Geneva: World Health Organisation Monograph

Boyd, C. and Sellers, L. (1982) *The British Way of Birth*, London: Pan

Boyle, M. (1992) The abortion debate, in P. Nicolson and J.M. Ussher (Eds) *The Psychology of Women's Health and Health Care*, London: Macmillan

Boyle, M. (1997) Making gender visible in clinical psychology, *Feminism and Psychology*, 7(2), 231–8

Brockington, I.F. and Kumar, R. (1982) *Motherhood and Mental Illness*, London: Academic Press

Brown, G. and Harris, T. (1978) *The Social Origins of Depression*, London: Tavistock

Burman, E. (1990) Differing with deconstruction, in I. Parker and J. Shotter (Eds) *Deconstructing Social Psychology*, London: Routledge

Burman, E. and Parker, I. (1993) *Discourse Analytic Research: Repertoires and Readings of Texts in Action*, London: Routledge

Burns, J. (1992) The psychology of lesbian health care, in P. Nicolson and J.M. Ussher (Eds) *The Psychology of Women's Health and Health Care*, London: Macmillan

Buss, D.M. (1994) The strategies of human mating, *American Scientist*, 82, 238–49

Caplan, P.J. and Caplan, J.B. (1994) *Thinking Critically about Research on Sex and Gender*, New York: HarperCollins

Cartwright, A. (1979) *The Dignity of Labour*, London: Tavistock

Changing the Subject Collective (1984) *Changing the Subject*, Eds J. Henriques, W. Holloway, C. Urwin, C. Venn and U.V. Walkerdine, London: Methuen

Chodorow, N. (1978) *The Reproduction of Mothering*, Berkeley: University of California Press

Chodorow, N. and Contratto, S. (1982) The fantasy of the perfect mother, in B. Thorne and M. Yalom (Eds) *Rethinking the Family: Some Feminist Questions*, New York: Longman

Choi, P.Y.L. (1994) Women's raging hormones, in P.Y.L. Choi and P. Nicolson (Eds) *Female Sexuality: Psychology, Biology and Social Context*, Hemel Hempstead: Harvester

Church, J. and Sommerfield, C. (1995) *Social Focus on Women*, Central Statistical Office, London: HMSO

Connell, R.W. (1993) *Gender and Power*, Cambridge: Polity Press

Cooper, C. and Lewis, S. (1993) *The Workplace Revolution: Managing Today's Dual Career Families*, London: Kogan Page

Coward, R. (1992) *Our Treacherous Hearts: Why Women Let Men Get their Own Way*, London: Faber and Faber

Cox, J.L. (1994) Introduction and classification dilemmas, in J. Cox and J. Holden (Eds) *Perinatal Psychiatry: Use and Misuse of the Edinburgh Postnatal Depression Scale*, London: Gaskell/ Royal College of Psychiatrists

Cox, J.L. and Holden, J. (Eds) (1994) *Perinatal Psychiatry: Use and Misuse of the Edinburgh Postnatal Depression Scale*, London: Gaskell/Royal College of Psychiatrists

Cox, J.L., Connor, Y.M., Henderson, I., McGuire, R.J. and Kendell, R.E. (1983) Prospective study of the psychiatric disorders of childbirth by self-report questionnaire, *Journal of Affective Disorders*, 5, 1–7

Cox, J.L., Connor, Y.M. and Kendell, R.E. (1982) Prospective study of the psychiatric disorders of childbirth, *British Journal of Psychiatry*, 140, 111–17

Coyle, A. and Wright, C. (1996) Using the counselling interview to collect research data on sensitive topics, *Journal of Health Psychology*, 1(4), 431–40

Crawford, M. and Maracek, J. (1989) Psychology reconstructs the female: 1968–1988, *Psychology of Women Quarterly*, 13, 147–66

Crouch, M. and Manderson, L. (1995) The social life of bonding theory, *Social Science and Medicine*, 41(6) 837–44

Dally, A. (1982) *Inventing Motherhood*, London: Burnett Books

Dalton, K. (1971) Prospective study into puerperal depression, *British Journal of Psychiatry*, 118, 689–92

Dalton, K. (1980/9 revised edition) *Depression after Childbirth*, Oxford: Oxford University Press.

Davidson, J.R.T. (1972) Postpartum mood change in Jamaican women: a description and discussion of its significance, *British Journal of Psychiatry*, 121, 659–63

Day, S. (1982) Is obstetric technology depressing? *Radical Science Journal*, 12, 659–63

Doherty, K. (1994) Subjectivity, reflexivity and the analysis of discourse, Paper presented at the British Psychological Society London Conference, University of London Institute of Education

Dosanj-Matwala, N. and Woollett, A. (1990) Asian women's ideas about contraception, family size and composition, *Journal of Reproductive and Infant Psychology*, 8, 231–2

Doyal, L. (1995) *What Makes Women Sick*, Basingstoke: Macmillan

Dryden, C. (1998) *Being Married, Doing Gender*, London: Routledge

Dunnewold, A. and Sanford, D.G. (1994) *Postpartum Survival Guide*, Oakland, CA: New Harbinger Publications

Eagley, A.H. (1987) *Sex Differences in Social Behaviour: A Social Role Interpretation*, Hillsdale: Earlbaum

Ehrenreich, B. and English, D. (1979) *For Her Own Good: 150 Years of the Experts' Advice to Women*, London: Pluto

Elliot, S.A. (1985) A rationale for psychosocial intervention in the prevention of postnatal depression, Paper presented at the first Women in Psychology Conference, Cardiff, South Wales

Elliot, S.A. (1990) Commentary on 'Childbirth as a life event', *Journal of Reproductive and Infant Psychology*, 8, 147–59

Elliot, S.A. (1994) Uses and misuses of the Edinburgh Postnatal Depression Scale in primary care: a comparison of models developed in health visiting, in J. Cox and J. Holden (Eds) *Perinatal Psychiatry: Use and Misuse of the Edinburgh Postnatal Depression Scale*, London: Gaskell/Royal College of Psychiatrists

Erikson, E. (1968/75) *Identity, Youth and Crisis*, London: Faber and Faber

Figes, K. (1994) *The Myth of Equality for Women in Britain*, Basingstoke: Macmillan

Foreman, D. (1994) Beyond the Edinburgh Postnatal Depression Scale: other rating scales and standardised interviews of use in assessing disturbed parents and their children, in J. Cox and J. Holden (Eds) *Perinatal Psychiatry: Use and Misuse of the Edinburgh Postnatal Depression Scale*, London: Gaskell/Royal College of Psychiatrists

Foucault, M. (1973) *The Archaeology of Knowledge*, London: Tavistock

Foucault, M. (1977) *Discipline and Punish*, London: Allen Lane

Foucault, M. (1980) *Power/Knowledge: Selected Interviews and Other Writings 1972–1977*, Brighton: Harvester Press

Frate, A.D. *et al.* (1979) Behavioural reactions during the post partum period, *Women and Health*, 4, 355–71

Friedan, B. (1963) *The Feminine Mystique*, London: Gollancz (1965) Harmondsworth: Penguin

Frommer, E.A. and O'Shea, G. (1973) The problems of childhood experience in relation to marriage and family building, *British Journal of Psychiatry*, 123, 157–60

Gannon, L. (1994) Sexuality and the menopause, in P.Y.L. Choi and P. Nicolson (Eds) *Female Sexuality: Psychology, Biology and Social Context*, Hemel Hempstead: Harvester Wheatsheaf.

Gavron, H. (1966/77) *The Captive Wife*, Harmondsworth: Penguin

Giddens, A. (1979) *Central Problems in Social Theory*, Basingstoke: Macmillan

Giddens, A. (1984) *The Constitution of Society*, Cambridge: Polity Press

Gillett, G. (1995) The philosophical foundations of qualitative psychology, *The Psychologist*, 8(3), 458–61

Gilligan, C. (1993) *In a Different Voice: Psychological Theory and Women's Development*, London: Harvard University Press

Gittins, D. (1993) *The Family in Question*, Basingstoke: Macmillan

Glaser, B. and Strauss, A. (1971) *Status Passage*, Chicago: Aldine

Gordon, R.E., Kapostins, E.E. and Gordon, K.K. (1965) Factors in postpartum emotional adjustment, *Obstetrics and Gynaecology*, 25, 158–66

Graham, H. and Oakley, A. (1981) Competing ideologies of reproduction, in H. Roberts (Ed.) *Women, Health and Reproduction*, London: RKP

Green, J.M. (1998) Post-natal depression or perinatal dysphoria? Findings from a longitudinal community-based study using the Edinburgh Postnatal Depression Scale, *Journal of Reproductive and Infant Psychology*, 16(1) (in press)

Griffin, C. (1986) Qualitative methods and female experience: young women from school to the job market, in S. Wilkinson (Ed.) *Feminist Social Psychology: Developing Theory and Practice*, Milton Keynes: Open University Press

Griffin, C. (1989) I'm not a women's libber but … feminism, consciousness and identity, in S. Skevington and D. Baker (Eds) *The Social Identity of Women*, London: Sage

Griffin, C. (1993) *Representations of Youth: The Study of Youth and Adolescence in Britain and America*, Cambridge: Polity Press

Harré, R. (1993) Foreword to J. Shotter, *Cultural Politics of Everyday Life*, Milton Keynes: Open University Press

Harré, R., Clarke, D. and DeCarlo, N. (1985) *Motives and Mechanisms: An Introduction to the Psychology of Action*, London: Methuen

Harré, R. and Gillett, G. (1994) *The Discursive Mind*, London: Sage

Harré, R. and Secord, P.F. (1972) *The Explanation of Social Behaviour*, Oxford: Blackwell.

Harris, B. (1981) Maternity blues in East African clinic attenders, *Archives of General Psychiatry*, 38, 1293–5

Hart, N. (1976) *When Marriage Ends*, London: Tavistock

Henderson, S. (1981) Social relationships, adversity and neurosis: an analysis of prospective observations, *British Journal of Psychiatry*, 138, 391–8

Henwood, K. and Nicolson, P. (1995) Qualitative research, *The Psychologist*, 8(3), 456–7

Henwood, K. and Pidgeon, N. (1995) Remaking the link: qualitative research and feminist standpoint theory, *Feminism and Psychology*, 5(1), 7–30

Hoeft, S.L. (1994) Is postnatal depression a normal response to the transition to motherhood? Unpublished dissertation, Department of Midwifery, University of Sheffield

Holden, J. (1985) Post natal depression: talking it out, *Community Outlook*, 6 and 10 October.

Holden, J. (1994) Can non-psychotic depression be prevented? in J. Cox and J. Holden (Eds) *Perinatal Psychiatry: Use and Misuse of the Edinburgh Postnatal Depression Scale*, London: Gaskell/Royal College of Psychiatrists

Hollway, W. (1989) *Subjectivity and Method in Psychology*, London: Sage

Hopkins, J., Marcus, M. and Campbell, S.B. (1984) Postpartum depression: a critical review, *Psychological Bulletin*, 95, 498–515

Huffman, L.C., Lamour, M., Bruan, Y.E. and Person, F.A. (1990) Depression symptomatology during pregnancy and postpartum: is the Beck Depression Inventory applicable? *Journal of Reproductive and Infant Psychology*, 8(2), 87–98

James, W. (1892) *Textbook of Psychology*, New York: Holt

Jelabi, C. (1993) A feminist perspective on post-natal depression, *Health Visitor*, 66(2), 59–60

Kaplan, M.M. (1992) *Mothers' Images of Motherhood*, London: Routledge

Katona, C.L. (1982) Puerperal mental illness: comparisons with non-puerperal controls, *British Journal of Psychiatry*, 141, 447–52

Kendell, R.E., MacKenzie, W.E., West, C., McGuire, R.J. and Cox, J.L. (1984) Day to day mood changes after childbirth: further data, *British Journal of Psychiatry*, 145, 620–25

Ketai, R.M. and Brandwin, M.A. (1979) Childbirth related psychosis and familial symbiotic conflict, *American Journal of Psychiatry*, 136, 190–3

Kitzinger, C. (1990) Resisting the discipline, in E. Burman (Ed.) *Feminists in Psychological Practice*, London: Sage

Kitzinger, S. (1975) *Some Mothers' Experience of Induced Labour*, London: National Childbirth Trust

Kitzinger, S. (1978) *Women as Mothers*, Glasgow: William Collins

Klaus, M. and Kennell, J.H. (1976) *Maternal Infant Bonding: The Impact of Early Separation and Loss on Family Development*, St Louis: C.V. Mosby

Kubler-Ross, E. (1970) *On Death and Dying*, London: Tavistock

Kumar, R. and Robson, K. (1978) Neurotic disturbance during pregnancy and the puerperium: preliminary report of a prospective survey of 119 primiparae, in M. Sandler (Ed.) *Mental Illness in Pregnancy and the Puerperium*, Oxford: Oxford Medical Publications

Lacan, J. (1949) The mirror stage as formative of the function of the 'I' in psychoanalytic experience. Reprinted in J. Lacan, *Ecrits: A Selection* (1977; trans. A. Sheridan), London: Tavistock

Lacan, J. (1977) *Ecrits: A Selection*, London: Tavistock

Leonard, P. (1984) *Personality and Ideology*, Basingstoke: Macmillan

Lewis, C. (1986) *Becoming a Father*, Milton Keynes: Open University Press

Lewis, S.E. (1995a) The social construction of depression: experience, discourse and subjectivity, Unpublished Ph.D. Thesis, University of Sheffield

Lewis, S.E. (1995b) A search for meaning: making sense of depression, *Journal of Mental Health*, 4, 369–82

Littlewood, J. and McHugh, N. (1997) *Maternal Distress and Postnatal Depression*, Basingstoke: Macmillan

Lyons, S. (1998) A prospective study of post traumatic stress symptoms one month following childbirth in a group of forty two first time mothers, *Journal of Reproductive and Infant Psychology*, 16(1) (in press)

McGuire, J. (1991) Sons and daughters, in A. Phoenix, A. Woollett and E. Lloyd (Eds) *Motherhood: Meanings, Practices and Ideologies*, London: Sage

Mandy, A., Gard, P.R., Ross, K. and Valentine, B.H. (1998) Psychological sequelae in women following either parturition or non-gynaecological surgery, *Journal of Reproductive and Infant Psychology*, 16(1) (in press)

Margison, F. (1990) Editorial: Special Issue on psychiatric disorders associated with childbearing, *Journal of Reproductive and Infant Psychology* 8(2), 63–6

Markova, I. (1985) Is evolutionary methodology a suitable alternative in applied social research?, Paper presented at the Social Psychology Section of the British Psychological Society's Annual Conference, Cambridge University

Marris, P. (1978) *Loss and Change*, London: Tavistock

Marshall, H. (1991) The social construction of motherhood: an analysis of childcare and parenting manuals, in A. Phoenix, A. Woollett and E. Lloyd. (Eds) *Motherhood: Meanings, Practices and Ideologies*, London: Sage

Marshall, J. (1986) Exploring the experiences of women managers: towards a rigour in qualitative methods, in S. Wilkinson (Ed.) *Feminist Social Psychology: Developing Theory and Practice*, Milton Keynes: Open University Press

Massarik, F. (1981) The interviewing process re-examined, in P. Reason and J. Rowan (Eds) *Human Inquiry: A Sourcebook of New Paradigm Research*, Chichester: Wiley

Mead, G H. (1934/67) *Mind, Self and Society*, Chicago: University of Chicago Press

Moscucci, O. (1993) *The Science of Woman: Gynaecology and Gender in England 1800–1929*, Cambridge: Cambridge University Press

Mueller, D. (1980) Social networks: a promising direction for research on the relationship of the social environment to psychiatric disorder, *Social Science and Medicine*, 14, 147–61

137

Munhall, P.L. (1994) *Qualitative Research: Proposals and Reports*, New York: National League for Nursing Press

Murray Parkes, C. (1971) Psychosocial transitions: a field for study, *Social Science and Medicine*, 5, 101–15.

Nicolson, P. (1983) Hospital midwives' perception of their roles and tasks, Paper presented at the annual conference of the Society for Reproductive and Infant Psychology, University of York

Nicolson, P. (1986) Developing a feminist approach to depression following childbirth, in S. Wilkinson (Ed.) *Feminist Social Psychology: Developing Theory and Practice*, Milton Keynes: Open University Press

Nicolson, P. (1988) The social psychology of post natal depression, Unpublished Ph.D. Thesis, University of London

Nicolson, P. (1990) A brief report of women's expectations of men's behaviour in the transition to parenthood, *Counselling Psychology Quarterly*, 2(4), 353–61

Nicolson, P. (1991) Virgins and wise women, Psychology of Women Section of the *British Psychological Society Newsletter*, 7, 5–8

Nicolson, P. (1992a) Towards a psychology of women's health and health care, in P. Nicolson and J. Ussher (Eds) *The Psychology of Women's Health and Health Care*, Basingstoke: Macmillan

Nicolson, P. (1992b) Menstrual cycle research and the construction of female psychology, in J.T.E. Richardson (Ed.) *Cognition and the Menstrual Cycle: Research, Theory and Culture*, London: Springer Verlag

Nicolson, P. (1993) Public values and private beliefs: why do women refer themselves for sex therapy?, in J.M. Ussher and C.D. Baker (Eds) *Psychological Perspectives on Sexual Problems*, London: Routledge

Nicolson, P. (1994) Reflexivity and the experience of the research interview: women's identity, self awareness and the case of post-natal depression. In the symposium, Health: the Psychology of Gender and the Experience of Self, Second International Interdisciplinary Qualitative Health Research Conference, Penn State University, USA.

Nicolson, P. (1995a) Qualitative research and mental health: analysing subjectivity, *Journal of Mental Health*, 4(4), 337–45

Nicolson, P. (1995b) Feminism and psychology, in J.A. Smith, R. Harré and L. Van Langenhove (Eds) *Rethinking Psychology*, London: Sage

Nicolson, P. and Ussher, J.M. (Eds) (1992) *The Psychology of Women's Health and Health Care*, Basingstoke: Macmillan

Nilsson, A. (1970) Para-natal emotional adjusment: a prospective study of 165 women, Part 1, *Acta Psychiatrica Scandinavica*, 47 (supp. 220), 1–61

Niven, C. (1992) *Psychological Care for Families: Before, during and after Birth*, Oxford: Butterworth Heinemann

Oakley, A. (1976) *Housewife*, Harmondsworth: Penguin

Oakley, A. (1979) The baby blues, *New Society*, 5 April, 11–12

Oakley, A. (1980) *Women Confined: Towards a Sociology of Childbirth*, Oxford: Martin Robertson

Oakley, A. (1981) *From Here to Maternity*, Harmondsworth: Pelican

Oakley, A. (1990) Who's afraid of the randomised control trial? Some dilemmas of the scientific method and 'good' research practice, in H. Roberts (Ed.) *Women's Health Counts*, London: Routledge

Oates, M. (1994) Postnatal mental illness: organisation and function of services, in J. Cox and J. Holden (Eds) *Perinatal Psychiatry: Use and Misuse of the Edinburgh Postnatal Depression Scale*, London: Gaskell/Royal College of Psychiatrists

O'Hara, M.W., Rehm, L.P. and Campbell, S.B. (1983) Postpartum depression: a role for social network and life stress variables, *Journal of Nervous and Mental Diseases*, 171, 336–41

OPCS (1995) *1993 Birth Statistics England and Wales*, London: HMSO

Parke, R.D. (1981) *Fathering*, Glasgow: Fontana

Parker, I. (1989) Discourse and power, in J. Shotter and K. Gergen (Eds) *Texts of Identity*, London: Sage

Parker, I. (1994) Qualitative research, in P. Banister, E. Burman, I. Parker, M. Taylor and C. Tindall (1994) *Qualitative Methods in Psychology: A Research Guide*, Buckingham: Open University Press

Parker, R. (1995) *Torn in Two: The Experience of Maternal Ambivalence*, London: Virago

Parsons, T. and Bales, R.F. (1953) *Family Socialization and Interaction Process*, New York: Free Press

Paykel, E.S., Emms, E.M., Fletcher, J. and Rassaby, E.S. (1980) Life events and social support in postnatal depression, *British Journal of Psychiatry*, 136, 339–46

Pearson, J. (1975) *The Deviant Imagination*, Basingstoke: Macmillan

Philp, M. (1985) Madness, truth and critique: Foucault and anti-psychiatry, *PsychCritique*, 1, 155–70

Phoenix, A. (1991) Mothers under twenty: the outsider and insider views, in A. Phoenix, A. Woollett and E. Lloyd (Eds) *Motherhood: Meanings, Practices and Ideologies*, London: Sage

Phoenix, A., Woollett, A. and Lloyd, E. (1991) *Motherhood: Meanings, Practices and Ideologies*, London: Sage

Pitt, B. (1968) 'Atypical' depression following childbirth, *British Journal of Psychiatry, 122*, 431–3

Pitt, B. (1978) Introduction, in M. Sandler (Ed.) *Mental Illness in Pregnancy and the Puerperium*, Oxford: Oxford Medical Publications

Pollock, S., Blurton Jones, N., Evans, M. and Woodson, E. (1980) Continuities in post natal depression, Paper presented at the British Psychological Society Special Conference on Childbirth, Leicester

Pope, C. and Mays, N. (1995) Researching the parts other methods cannot reach: an introduction to qualitative methods in health and health services research, *British Medical Journal*, 311, 42–5

Potter, J. and Wetherell, M. (1987) *Discourse and Social Psychology*, London: Sage

Rantzen, E. (1982) Introduction to C. Boyd and L. Sellers *The British Way of Birth*, London: Pan

Rapoport, A., Guyer, M.J. and Gordon, G. (1976) *2 x 2 Game*, Ann Arbor: University of Michigan Press

Rapoport, R. and Rapoport, R. (1976) *Dual Career Families Re-visited*, London: Martin Robertson

Reamy, K.J. and White, S.E. (1987) Sexuality in the puerperium: a review, *Archives of Sexual Behaviour*, 16(2), 165–87

Reinhartz, S. (1985) Feminist distrust: problems of context and content in sociological work, in D.N. Berg and K.K. Smith (Eds) *The Self in Social Inquiry: Researching Methods*, Newbury Park, California: Sage

Revans, R.W. (1968) *Standards for Morale: Cause and Effect in Hospital*, Oxford: Nuffield Provincial Hospital Trust

Rich, A. (1977/84) *Of Woman Born*, London: Virago

Richardson, D. (1993) *Women, Motherhood and Childrearing*, Basingstoke: Macmillan

Richardson, J.T.E. (Ed.) (1992) *Cognition and the Menstrual Cycle: Research, Theory and Culture*, London: Springer Verlag

Riger, S. (1992) Epistemological debates, feminist voices: science, social values, and the study of women, *American Psychologist*, 47(6), 730–40

Riley, D. (1983) *The War in the Nursery: Theories of the Child and Mother*, London: Virago

Rose, N. (1985) *The Psychological Complex*, London: RKP

Rosenwald, G.C. *et al.* (1972) Early and late post partum illnesses, *Psychosomatic Medicine*, 34, 129–37

Rossan, S. (1987) Changes in the marital relationship during pregnancy and early motherhood, Paper presented at the second Women and Psychology Conference, Brunel University

Rowan, J. (1981) From anxiety to method in the behavioural sciences by George Devereaux: an appreciation, in P. Reason and J. Rowan (Eds) *Human Inquiry: A Sourcebook of New Paradigm Research*, Chichester: Wiley

Rubin, H.J. and Rubin, I.S. (1995) *Qualitative Interviewing: The Art of Hearing Data*, London: Sage

Ruddick, S. (1982) Maternal thinking, in B. Thorne and M. Yalom (Eds) *Rethinking the Family: Some Feminist Questions*, London: Longman

Sampson, E.E. (1993) *Celebrating the other: A Dialogic Account of Human Nature*, Boulder, CO: Westview Press

Sayers, J. (1988) Feminist therapy: forgetting the father?, in the Psychology of Women Section of the *British Psychological Society Newsletter*, 2, 18–22

Segal, L. (1990) *Slow Motion: Changing Masculinities Changing Men*, London: Virago

Sharpe, S. (1976) *Just Like a Girl*, Harmondsworth: Penguin

Sharpe, S. (1994) *Just Like a Girl: From the Seventies to the Nineties*, Harmondsworth: Penguin

Sherif, C.(1987) Bias in psychology, in S. Harding (Ed.) *Feminism and Methodology*, Milton Keynes: Open University Press

Shorter, E. (1984) *A History of Women's Bodies*, Harmondsworth: Pelican

Shotter, J. (1993) *Cultural Politics of Everyday Life*, Milton Keynes: Open University Press

Showalter, E. (1978) *The Female Malady*, London: Virago

Sluckin, W., Herbert, M. and Sluckin, A. (1983) *Maternal Bonding*, Oxford: Basil Blackwell

Smith, J.A. (1992) Pregnancy and the transition to motherhood, in P. Nicolson and J.M. Ussher (Eds) *The Psychology of Women's Health and Health Care*, London: Macmillan

Smith, J.A. (1993) Persons, text and talk: subjectivity, reflexivity and qualitative research in psychology, Paper presented at the BPS Social Psychology Section Conference, University of Oxford

Sneddon, J. (1982) Is puerperal psychosis an entity after all?, Paper presented at the Marcé Society Conference, Institute of Psychiatry, London

Stanley, L. and Wise, S. (1983) *Breaking Out: Feminist Consciousness and Feminist Research*, London: Routledge and Kegan Paul

Steier, F. (Ed.) (1991) *Research and Reflexivity*, London: Sage

Steiner, M. (1979) Psychobiology of mental disorders associated with childbearing: an overview, *Acta Psychiatrica Scandinavica*, 60, 449–64

Tew, M. (1978) The case against hospital deliveries, in S. Kitzinger and J. Davis (Eds) *The Place of Birth*, Oxford: Oxford University Press

Thurtle, V. (1995) Post-natal depression: the relevance of sociological approaches, *Journal of Advanced Nursing*, 22, 416–24

Tizard, B. (1991) Employed mothers and the care of young children, in A. Phoenix, A. Woollett and E. Lloyd (Eds) *Motherhood: Meanings, Practices and Ideologies*, London: Sage

Tod, E.D.M. (1964) Puerperal depression: a prospective epidemiological study, *The Lancet*, 2, 1264–6

Tunaley, J.R. (1995) Body size, food and women's identity: a lifespan approach, Unpublished Ph.D. Thesis, University of Sheffield

Urwin, C. (1984) Power relations and emergence of language, in J. Henriques, W. Holloway, C. Urwin, C. Venn and U.V. Walkerdine (Eds) *Changing the Subject*, London: Methuen

Ussher, J.M. (1989) *The Psychology of the Female Body*, London: Routledge and Kegan Paul

Ussher, J.M. (1991) *Women's Madness: Misogyny or Mental Illness?* London: Harvester Wheatsheaf

Ussher, J.M. (1992) Reproductive rhetoric and the blaming of the body, in P. Nicolson and J.M. Ussher (Eds) *The Psychology of Women's Health and Health Care*, London: Macmillan

Watson, M. and Foreman, D. (1994) Diminishing the impact of puerperal neuroses: towards an expressive psychotherapy useful in a community setting, in J. Cox and J. Holden (Eds) *Perinatal Psychiatry: Use and Misuse of the Edinburgh Postnatal Depression Scale*, London: Gaskell/Royal College of Psychiatrists

Weedon, C. (1987) *Feminist Practice and Poststructuralist Theory*, Oxford: Blackwell

Whiffen, V.E. (1992) Is postnatal depression a distinct diagnosis? *Clinical Psychology Review*, 12, 485–508

World Health Organisation (1992) *The ICD-10 Classification of Mental and Behavioural Disorder*, Geneva: WHO

Wilkinson, S.J. (1986) *Feminist Social Psychology: Theory and Method*, Milton Keynes: Open University Press

Wilkinson, S.J. (Ed.) (1996) *Feminist Social Psychologies: International Perspectives*, Milton Keynes: Open University Press

Woollett, A. (1987) Why motherhood is popular: an analysis of accounts of mothers and childless women, Paper presented at the second Women and Psychology Conference, Brunel University, Uxbridge

Woollett, A. (1991) Having children: accounts of childless women and women with reproductive problems, in A. Phoenix, A. Woollett and E. Lloyd (Eds) *Motherhood: Meanings, Practices and Ideologies*, London: Sage

Woollett, A. (1992) Psychological aspects of infertility and infertility investigation, in P. Nicolson and J.M. Ussher (Eds) *The Psychology of Women's Health and Health Care*, London: Macmillan

York, R. (1990) Pattern of postpartum blues, *Journal of Reproductive and Infant Psychology* 8(2), 67–74

Young, M. and Wilmott, P. (1966) *Family and Kinship in East London*, Harmondsworth: Penguin

AUTHOR INDEX

SUBJECT INDEX

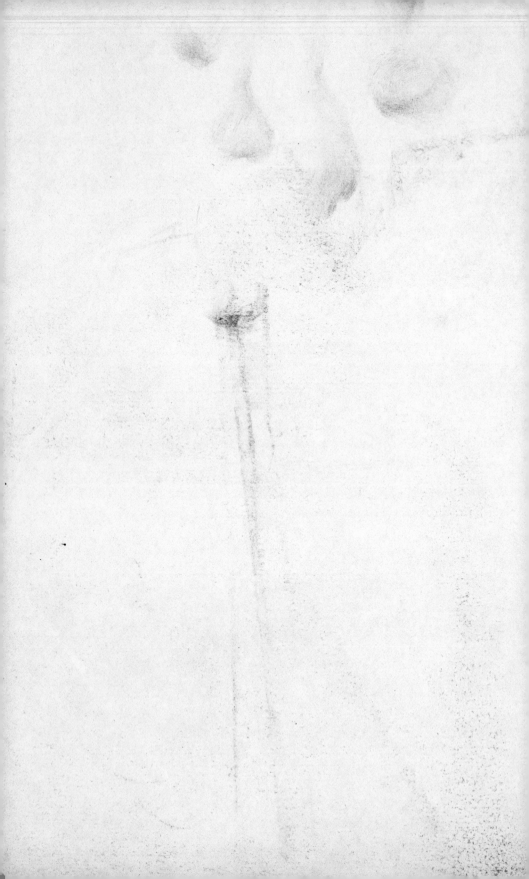